GRANNY CROCHET
Favorites

BY JEAN LEINHAUSER & RITA WEISS

Sterling Publishing Co., Inc.   New York

Book design by CBG Graphics
Carol Belanger Grafton, designer

Copyright © 1989 by Jean Leinhauser and Rita Weiss
Published by Sterling Publishing Co., Inc.
387 Park Avenue South, New York, N.Y. 10016
Distributed in Canada by Sterling Publishing
℅ Canadian Manda Group, P.O. Box 920, Station U
Toronto, Ontario, Canada M8Z 5P9
Distributed in Great Britain and Europe by Cassell PLC
Artillery House, Artillery Row, London SW1P 1RT, England
Distributed in Australia by Capricorn Ltd.
P.O. Box 665, Lane Cove, NSW 2066

Sterling ISBN 0-8069-6540-1

INTRODUCTION

The lowly granny square—the easiest, quickest, most portable and most fun form of crochet—is the star of this book.

The granny can be dressed up to look like a flower, or worked in a rainbow of colors; it can be a square, a circle or a hexagon; or it can be very traditional.

We are both lovers of the granny, and delight in finding new versions and new ways to use it. This is our first hardcover book devoted entirely to grannies— and we hope not the last.

We've done designs in crochet thread, in worsted, sport and baby weight yarn; we've used up scraps, we've bought all new yarn. We've created warm afghans, fashionable clothes, kitchen accessories, children's things—even a dog coat. If there's anything that can't be made with a granny, we haven't found it yet!

Do you have a pattern for a unique granny square or motif? If you're willing to share, send it along to us and we'll try to use it in the next book.

1455 Linda Vista Drive
San Marcos, CA 92069

Jean Leinhauser
Rita Weiss

For Sabrina and Michelle,
who turned me into a granny
[RW]

For my sister, Caroline Oster,
dear friend and favorite playmate
[JL]

ACKNOWLEDGMENTS

Coats & Clark and Caron International kindly let us use two of their designs, and graciously lent us the color photographs of the finished projects.

Special thanks to a group of women whose fingers flew making models and testing patterns so that we could meet our deadlines: Carolyn Hawkins and Miriam Dow of Vista, CA; Hannelore Southard of San Marcos, CA; Jane Carter, who is very mobile but often found in Bodfish, CA.

Staff
Mary Ann Frits, Editor
Linda Walker, Pattern Writer
Candy Matthews, Project Coordinator
Marlene Bressler, Diagrams

CONTENTS

Chapter 6: GRANNY'S GIFTS 125

INDEX 143

Chapter 1
GRANNY TECHNIQUES

Even beginning crocheters find granny motifs easy and fun. Before beginning to crochet any of our projects, please read through this chapter to refresh your memory or practice a technique.

Granny's Recipes

Practice Square

If you've never made a granny motif, following are instructions for a basic square that will help you learn the techniques. However, when making a specific project in this book or any other source, follow the exact instructions given, as there are many different ways of making a granny motif. To work the square, you'll need a few yards of several different colors, and a size H aluminum crochet hook.

Make a sl knot on hook with first color (**Fig 1**), leaving a 4″ end. Ch 4, join with a sl st to form a ring (**Fig 2**).

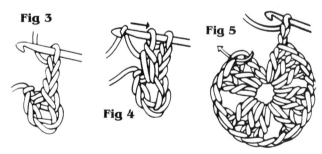

Rnd 1: [On this round, you will be working *into* the ring. As you do this, also work over the 4″ end left after making the sl knot; this keeps down the number of yarn ends to be run in after the square is completed.] Ch 3 (**Fig 3**), 2 dc in ring (**Fig 4**) shows first dc being worked in ring); (ch 2, 3 dc in ring) 3 times; ch 2, join in 3rd ch of beg ch-3 with a sl st (**Fig 5**). [The side of the work now facing you is called the *right* side of the work.] Finish off first color.

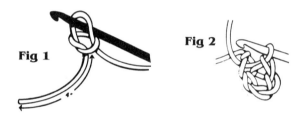

Rnd 2: Make a sl knot on hook with 2nd color; with right side of work facing you, join 2nd color with a sl st in any ch-2 sp (these are corner sps); ch 3, 2 dc in same sp (**Fig 6** shows first dc being worked in sp); ch 2, 3 dc again in same sp; * in next ch-2 sp, work (3 dc, ch 2, 3 dc); rep from * twice, join with a sl st in 3rd ch of beg ch-3. Finish off 2nd color. Look at your work; you should now have a perfect square.

Rnd 3: With right side of work facing you, join 3rd color as before in any ch-2 corner sp; (ch 3, 2 dc, ch 2, 3 dc) all in same sp; between next two 3-dc groups (**Fig 7**), work 3 dc for side; * (3 dc, ch 2, 3 dc) all in next ch-2 sp for corner; 3 dc between next two 3-dc groups for side; rep from * twice, join with a sl st in 3rd ch of beg ch-3. Finish off 3rd color.

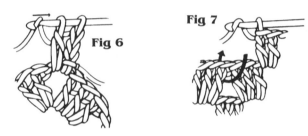

Rnd 4: With right side of work facing you, join 4th color as before in any ch-2 corner sp; (ch 3, 2 dc, ch 2, 3 dc) all in same sp; * (3 dc between next two 3-dc groups) twice for side; (3 dc, ch 2, 3 dc) all in next ch-2 sp for corner; rep from * twice; (3 dc between next two 3-dc groups) twice for side; join with a sl st in 3rd ch of beg ch-3. Finish off 4th color. Weave in all loose yarn ends; trim them off.

Notes

1. You now have a 4-rnd square; work any additional desires rnds as for Rnd 4, working one more side group of 3 dcs on every additional rnd.

2. Unless a pattern specifies that you must *turn* your work before each new rnd, always work with the right side facing you.

3. When a pattern calls for working 2 or more rnds of the same color in succession, work to end of rnd, join, but do not finish off. Sl st in tops of each of next 2 dcs and into corner sp; work next rnd as specified.

4. When making grannys, you'll have lots of yarn ends to weave in (do this securely). Make it a practice to weave these in as you finish each square, unless the pattern says not to.

Gauge

This is the most important aspect of crochet—if you don't work to gauge, your crocheted projects will never be the correct size, and you may not have enough yarn to finish your project.

Gauge means the number of stitches per inch, and rows per inch, that result from a specified yarn

worked with a specified size hook. But since everyone crochets differently—some loosely, some tightly, some in between—the measurements of individual work can vary greatly when using the same size hook and yarn. It is your responsibility to make sure you achieve the gauge specified in the pattern.

Hook sizes given in instructions are merely guides and should never be used without making a sample square to check gauge. Do not hesitate to change to a larger or smaller size hook if necessary to achieve gauge. If you get a smaller square than specified, try again with a larger size hook. If you get a bigger square than specified, try again with a smaller size hook. Keep trying until you find the size hook that will give you the specified gauge.

If you have the correct number of stitches per inch, but cannot achieve the row gauge, adjust the height of your stitches. This means that after inserting the hook to begin a new stitch, draw up a little more yarn if your stitches are not tall enough—this makes the first loop slightly higher; or draw up less yarn if your stitches are too tall. Practice will help you achieve the correct height.

Joining

When joining granny squares or other pieces of crochet, we often tell you to sew through back loops only. Do this with an overcast stitch, working through the outer loops as shown in **Fig 8**. Take care not to pull the sewing stitches too tightly.

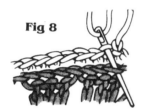

Fig 8

Edgings

Single Crochet Edging: Upon completion of a project, it is sometimes necessary to finish an edge. The instructions will say to "work a row of single crochet, taking care to keep work flat." This means to adjust your stitches as you work. You may need to skip a row or stitch here or there to keep the edging from rippling; or add a stitch to keep the work from pulling in. When working around a corner, it is usually necessary to work 3 stitches in the center corner stitch to keep the corner flat and square.

Reverse Single Crochet Edging: This edging produces a lovely corded effect and is usually worked after a row of single crochet. It is worked on the right side **from left to right** (the opposite direction for working single crochet). Work one reverse single crochet in each stitch across (see **Figs 9 and 10**).

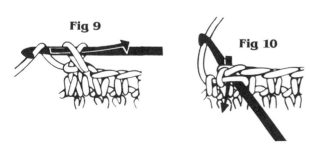

Fig 9

Fig 10

Fringe

Basic Instructions

Cut a piece of cardboard about 6″ wide and half as long as specified in instructions for strands plus ½″ for trimming allowance. Wind yarn loosely and evenly lengthwise around cardboard. When card is filled, cut yarn across one end. Do this several times, then begin fringing; you can wind additional strands as you need them.

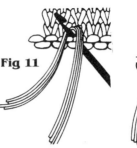

Fig 11

Fig 12

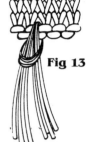

Fig 13

Single Knot Fringe

Hold specified number of strands for one knot of fringe together, then fold in half. Hold afghan with right side facing you. Use crochet hook to draw folded end through space or stitch from right to wrong side (**Figs 11 and 12**), pull loose ends through folded section (**Fig 13**) and draw knot up firmly (**Fig 14**). Space knots as indicated in pattern instructions. Trim ends of fringe evenly.

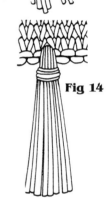

Fig 14

Spaghetti Fringe

Each knot is tied with just one strand of yarn. Use same knotting method as for Single Knot Fringe.

Double Knot Fringe

Begin by working Single Knot Fringe completely across one end of afghan. With right side facing you and working from left to right, take half the strands of one knot and half the strands in the knot next to it, and knot them together (**Fig 15**).

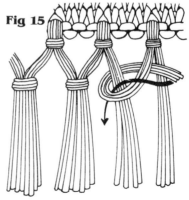

Fig 15

Fig 16

Triple Knot Fringe

First work Double Knot Fringe. Then working again on right side from left to right, tie third row of knots as in **Fig. 16**.

Granny's Special Shorthand

Symbols

* An asterisk is used to mark the beginning of a portion of instructions which will be worked more than once; thus, "rep from * twice" means after working the instructions once, repeat the instructions following the asterisk twice more (3 times in all).

† The dagger identifies a portion of instructions that will be repeated again later in the pattern.

: The number after a colon at the end of a row indicates the number of stitches you should have when the row has been completed.

( ) Parentheses are used to enclose instructions which should be worked the exact number of times specified immediately following the parentheses, such as (2 sc in next dc, sc in next dc) twice. They are also used to set off and clarify a group of sts that are to be worked all into the same sp or st, such as (2 dc, ch 1, 2 dc) in corner sp.

[ ] Brackets and ( ) parentheses are used to provide additional information to clarify instructions.

Abbreviations

Most of the terms used in this book are the same as the English ones. Terms which have different English equivalents are noted below.

Term	American	English
beg **bl(s)** **ch(s)**	begin(ning) back loop(s) chain(s)	
dec **dc** **dtrc** **Fig**	decrease (-ing) double crochet(s) double triple crochet figure	treble (tr)
fl(s)	front loop(s)	
hdc	half double crochet(s)	half treble (htr)
inc **patt** **prev** **rem** **rep** **rnd(s)**	increase (-ing) pattern previous remain(ing) repeat(ing) round(s)	
sc	single crochet(s)	double crochet (dc)
sk	skip	miss
sl	slip	
sl st(s)	slip stitch(es)	slip stitch (ss) (or "single crochet")
sp(s) **st(s)** **tog**	space(s) stitch(es) together	
trc	triple crochet(s)	double treble (dtr)
YO	yarn over	yarn round hook (yrh)

Crochet Hooks

The sizing of American crochet hooks is different from the English. American hook sizes with their English equivalent are given here.

American	English
K	7mm
J	6mm
I	5.50mm
H	5mm
G	4.50mm
F	4mm

American	English
E	3.50mm
D	3mm
C	2.50mm
B	2mm
O (steel)	2.50mm
7 (steel)	1.50mm

Yarns Used In This Book

American	English
Worsted weight	Double knitting weight
Sport weight	4-ply weight
Baby weight	3-ply weight
Bedspread weight	Lightweight crochet cotton

Note: These are approximate equivalents only; it is therefore most important that you check your tension before you begin the main work. Make a 4-inch square of the pattern and, if you cannot get the correct gauge with the needles or hook quoted, experiment with smaller or larger sizes until you find the correct size to use. The quantities of yarn given are also approximate and if you change the needle or hook size, you may find you need a little extra yarn. Bear this in mind when buying the yarn, so that you have the same dye lot to complete your work.

Terms

join—join yarn with a sl st, unless otherwise specified

back loops—those away from you

front loops—those toward you

inner loops—the front loop on the piece away from you, and the **back loop on the piece toward you** (used when joining)

outer loops—the back loop on the square away from you, and the **front loop on the square toward you** (used when joining squares)

gauge—tension (English equivalent)

A Treasury of Granny Squares

Several granny squares are used in many projects in this book. We are giving the instructions for them here, and individual patterns will refer you to this section.

Traditional Granny Square #1

This is a multi-colored square.

With Color A, ch 4, join to form a ring.

Rnd 1: Ch 3 (counts as a dc in this and all following rnds), 2 dc in ring; (ch 2, 3 dc in ring) 3 times; ch 2; join in 3rd ch of beg ch-3; finish off. Do not turn; work in rnds.

Rnd 2: Join color B in any ch-2 sp; ch 3, in same sp work (2 dc, ch 2, 3 dc): corner made; * ch 1, sk next 3 dc, in next ch-2 sp work (3 dc, ch 2, 3 dc): corner made; rep from * twice more; ch 1, sk next 3 dc; join in 3rd ch of beg ch-3; finish off.

Rnd 3: Join color C in any ch-2 corner sp; ch 3, in same sp work (2 dc, ch 2, 3 dc): corner made; * ch 1, sk next 3 dc, sk next 3 dc, 3 dc in next ch-1 sp: 3-dc group made; ch 1, sk next 3 dc, in next ch-2 corner sp work (3 dc, ch 2, 3 dc): corner made; rep from * twice more; ch 1, 3 dc in next ch-1 sp: 3-dc group made; ch 1, sk next 3 dc; join in 3rd ch of beg ch-3; finish off.

Rnd 4: Join color D in any ch-2 corner sp; ch 3, in same sp work (2 dc, ch 2, 3 dc): corner made; * (ch 1, sk next 3 dc, 3 dc in next ch-1 sp) twice; ch 1, sk next 3 dc, in next ch-2 corner sp work (3 dc, ch 2, 3 dc): corner made; rep from * twice more; (ch 1, sk next 3 dc, 3 dc in next ch-1 sp) twice; ch 1, sk next 3 dc; join in 3rd ch of beg ch-3; finish off.

Rep Rnd 4 for squares requiring more rnds. Each successive rnd will have one additional (ch 1, 3-dc group) between corners.

Traditional Granny Half Square

With Color A, ch 4, join to form a ring.

Row 1 (right side): Ch 3 (counts as a dc in this and all following rows), 2 dc in ring, ch 2: corner sp made; 3 dc in ring; finish off Color A.

Note: All following rows are worked on right side.

Row 2: With right side facing you, join Color B in 3rd ch of beg ch-3 of prev row; ch 3, 2 dc in same st: 3-dc group made; ch 1, sk next 2 dc, in ch-2 corner sp work (3 dc, ch 2, 3 dc): corner made; ch 1, sk next 2 dc, 3 dc in last dc: 3-dc group made; finish off: 1, 3-dc group on each side of corner sp.

Row 3: Join Color C in 3rd ch of beg ch-3 of prev row; ch 3, 2 dc in same st as joining: 3-dc group made; ch 1, sk next 2 dc, 3 dc in next ch-1 sp: 3-dc group made; ch 1, sk next 3 dc, in next ch-2 sp work (3 dc, ch 2, 3 dc): corner made; ch 1, sk next 3 dc, 3 dc in next ch-1 sp: 3-dc group made; ch 1, sk next 2 dc, 3 dc in last dc: 3-dc group made: 2, 3-dc groups on each side of corner sp; finish off Color C.

Row 4: Join Color D in 3rd ch of beg ch-3 of prev row, ch 3, 2 dc in same st as joining: 3-dc group made; ch 1, (sk next 3-dc group, 3 dc in next ch-1 sp, ch 1) twice; sk next 3-dc group, in corner sp work (3 dc, ch 2, 3 dc): corner made; ch 1, (sk next 3-dc group, 3 dc in next ch-1 sp, ch 1) twice; sk next 2 dc, 3 dc in last dc: 3-dc group made: 3, 3-dc groups on each side of corner sp; finish off.

Rep Rnd 4 for squares requiring more rnds. Each successive rnd will have one additional (ch 1, 3-dc group) on each side of corner sp.

Traditional Granny Square #2

This is the Traditional Granny Square #1 made with one color instead of various colors.

With color A, ch 4, join to form a ring.

Rnd 1: Ch 3 (counts as a dc in this and all following rnds), 2 dc in ring; (ch 2, 3 dc in ring) 3 times; ch 2; join in 3rd ch of beg ch-3. Do not turn; work in rnds.

Rnd 2: Sl st in next 2 dc and ch-2 sp; ch 3, in same sp work (2 dc, ch 2, 3 dc): corner made; * ch 1, sk next 3 dc, in next ch-2 sp work (3 dc, ch 2, 3 dc): corner made; rep from * twice more; ch 1, sk next 3 dc; join in 3rd ch of beg ch-3.

Rnd 3: Sl st in next 2 dc and ch-2 corner sp; ch 3, in same sp work (2 dc, ch 2, 3 dc): corner made; * ch 1, sk next 3 dc, 3 dc in next ch-1 sp: 3-dc group made; ch 1, sk next 3 dc, in next ch-2 corner sp work (3 dc, ch 2, 3 dc): corner made; rep from * twice more; ch 1, sk next 3 dc, 3 dc in next ch-1 sp: 3-dc group made; ch 1, sk next 3 dc; join in 3rd ch of beg ch-3.

Rnd 4: Sl st in next 2 dc and ch-2 corner sp; ch 3, in same sp work (2 dc, ch 2, 3 dc): corner made; * (ch 1, sk next 3 dc, 3 dc in next ch-1 sp) twice; ch 1, sk next 3 dc, in next ch-2 corner sp work (3 dc, ch 2, 3 dc): corner made; rep from * twice more; (ch 1, sk next 3 dc, 3 dc in next ch-1 sp) twice; ch 1, sk next 3 dc; join in 3rd ch of beg ch-3; finish off.

For squares requiring more rnds, do not finish off at end of Rnd 4. Rep Rnd 4 the required number of times then finish off. Each successive rnd will have one additional (ch 1, 3-dc group) between corners.

Puff Granny Square

With Color A, ch 5, join to form a ring.

Rnd 1: Ch 3 (counts as a dc), 15 dc in ring; join in 3rd ch of beg ch-3: 16 dc; finish off Color A.

Rnd 2: Join Color B between any 2 dc; ch 5 (counts as a dc and ch 2); (dc between next 2 dc, ch 2) 15 times; join in 3rd ch of beg ch-5: 16 ch-2 sps; finish off Color B.

Rnd 3: Join Color C in any ch-2 sp; (YO, insert hook in same sp, YO and draw up a ¼″ lp) 4 times: 9 lps on hook; YO and draw through 8 lps; YO and draw through 2 rem lps on hook: puff st made; * ch 2, in next ch-2 sp work puff st; rep from * 14 times more; ch 2; join in top of first puff st: 16 puff sts; finish off Color C.

Rnd 4: Join Color D in any ch-2 sp; ch 4 (counts as a trc), in same sp work (2 trc, ch 1, 3 trc): corner made; * (ch 1, 2 dc in next ch-2 sp) 3 times, ch 1; in next ch-2 sp work (3 trc, ch 1, 3 trc): corner made; rep from * twice more; (ch 1, 2 dc in next ch-2 sp) 3 times; ch 1; join in 4th ch of beg ch-4: 3, 2-dc groups between corners; finish off and weave in ends.

Log Cabin Square

With Color A, ch 2.

Rnd 1: 4 sc in 2nd ch from hook. Do not join and do not turn; work in spiral, marking beg of rnds.

Rnd 2: (3 sc in next sc) 4 times: 12 sc.

Rnd 3: (3 sc in next sc, sc in next 2 sc) 4 times: 4 corners with 2 sc between.

Rnd 4: Sc in next sc; (3 sc in next sc, sc in next 4 sc) 3 times; 3 sc in next sc, sc in next 3 sc.

Rnd 5: Sc in next 2 sc; (3 sc in next sc, sc in next 6 sc) 3 times; 3 sc in next sc, sc in next 4 sc.

Rnd 6: Sc in next 3 sc; (3 sc in next sc, sc in next 8 sc) 3 times; 3 sc in next sc, sc in next 5 sc.

Rnd 7: Sc in next 4 sc; (3 sc in next sc, sc in next 10 sc) 3 times; 3 sc in next sc, sc in next 6 sc.

Rnd 8: Sc in next 5 sc, draw lp of Color B through last sc, drop Color A; (3 sc in next sc, sc in next 12 sc) 3 times; 3 sc in next sc, sc in next 12 sc, working through marked beg st of rnd to corner; finish off Color B and cut Color A.

Rnd 9: Join Color C in center sc of any corner; ch 3 (counts as dc), in same sc work (dc, ch 2, 2 dc): corner made;* † ch 1, (sk 2 sc, 2 dc in next sc, ch 1) 4 times †; sk 2 sc, in next sc work (2 dc, ch 2, 2 dc): corner made; rep from * twice more, then rep from † to † once; sk 2 sc; join in 3rd ch of beg ch-3; finish off Color C.

Rnd 10: Join Color A in any ch-2 corner sp; ch 1, 3 sc in same sp: corner made; * (sc in next 2 dc, sc in ch-1 sp) 5 times; sc in next 2 dc, 3 sc in next ch-2 sp: corner made; rep from * 3 times more, ending last rep without working last 3 sc: 17 sc between corners; sc in next sc.

Rnd 11: (3 sc in next sc, sc in next 19 sc) 4 times: 19 sc between corners; sc in next sc, sl st in next sc; finish off and weave in ends.

Wagon Wheel Square #1

With Color A, ch 8, join to form a ring.

Rnd 1: Ch 3 (counts as a dc), 15 dc in ring: 16 dc; join in 3rd ch of beg ch-3. Do not turn; work in rnds.

Rnd 2: Sl st between ch-3 and next dc, ch 5 (counts as a dc and ch 2); (dc between next 2 dc, ch 2) 15 times; join in 3rd ch of beg ch-5: 16 ch-2 sps.

Rnd 3: Sl st in next ch-2 sp, ch 3 (counts as a dc), 2 dc in same sp, ch 1; (3 dc in next ch-2 sp, ch 1) 15 times; join in 3rd ch of beg ch-3: 16 ch-1 sps; finish off Color A.

Rnd 4: Join Color B in any ch-1 sp; * (ch 3, sc in next ch-1 sp) 3 times; ch 5, sc in next ch-1 sp: corner made; rep from * 3 times more, ending last rep without working last sc; join in beg sl st: 4 corners with 3 ch-3 sps between.

Rnd 5: Sl st in next ch-3 sp; ch 3 (counts as a dc), 2 dc in same sp; (3 dc in next ch-3 sp) twice; * in next ch-5 corner sp work (3 dc, ch 2, 3 dc): corner made; (3 dc in next ch-3 sp) 3 times; rep from * twice more; in next ch-5 corner sp work (3 dc, ch 2, 3 dc): corner made; join in 3rd ch of beg ch-3; finish off Color B.

Rnd 6: Join Color C in any ch-2 corner sp; ch 3 (counts as a dc), in same sp work (trc, dc): corner made; * (dc between next 2 dc) 14 times; in next ch-2 corner sp work (dc, trc, dc): corner made; rep from * 3 times more, ending last rep without working last (dc, trc, dc); join in 3rd ch of beg ch-3; finish off Color C and weave in ends.

Wagon Wheel Square #2

With Color A, ch 8, join to form a ring.

Rnd 1: Ch 3 (counts as a dc), 15 dc in ring; join in 3rd ch of beg ch-3: 16 dc. Do not turn; work in rnds.

Rnd 2: Sl st between ch-3 and next dc; ch 5 (counts as a dc and ch 2); (dc between next 2 dc, ch 2) 15 times; join in 3rd ch of beg ch-5: 16 ch-2 sps.

Rnd 3: Sl st in next ch-2 sp, ch 3 (counts as a dc), 2 dc in same sp; ch 1, (3 dc in next ch-2 sp, ch 1) 15 times; join in 3rd ch of beg ch-3: 16 ch-1 sps; finish off.

Rnd 4: Join Color B in any ch-1 sp; * (ch 3, sc in next ch-1 sp) 3 times; ch 5, sc in next ch-1 sp: corner made; rep from * 3 times more, ending last rep without working last sc; join in beg sl st: 4 corners with 3 ch-3 sps between.

Rnd 5: Sl st in next ch-3 sp; ch 3 (counts as a dc in this and following rnd), 2 dc in same sp; (3 dc in next ch-3 sp) twice; * in next ch-5 sp work (5 dc, ch 2, 5 dc): corner made; (3 dc in next ch-3 sp) 3 times; rep from * twice more; in next ch-5 sp work (5 dc, ch 2, 5 dc): corner made; join in 3rd ch of beg ch-3: 3, 3-dc groups between corners; finish off Color B.

Rnd 6: Join Color C in any ch-2 corner sp; ch 3, in same sp work (trc, dc): corner made; dc in next 19 dc; * in next ch-2 corner sp work (dc, trc, dc): corner made; dc in next 19 dc; rep from * twice more; join in 3rd ch of beg ch-3; finish off and weave in ends.

Wagon Wheel Square #3

With Color A, ch 8, join to form a ring.

Rnd 1: Ch 3 (counts as a dc), 15 dc in ring; join in 3rd ch of beg ch-3: 16 dc.

Rnd 2: Ch 4 (counts as a dc and ch 1), (dc in next dc, ch 1)15 times; join in 3rd ch of beg ch-4: 16 ch-1 sps.

Rnd 3: Sl st in next ch-1 sp, ch 3 (counts as a dc), 2 dc in same sp, ch 1; (sk next 3 dc, 3 dc in next ch-1 sp, ch 1) 15 times; 16 ch-1 sps; finish off Color A.

Rnd 4: Join Color B in any ch-1 sp, ch 1, sc in same sp; * (ch 3, sk next 3 dc, sc in next ch-1 sp) 3 times; ch 5, sk next 3 dc, sc in next ch-1 sp: corner sp made; rep from * 3 times

more; (ch 3, sk next 3 dc, sc in next ch-1 sp) 3 times; ch 5, sk next 3 dc; join in first sc: 4 ch-5 corner sps.

Rnd 5: Sl st in next ch-3 sp; ch 3 (counts as a dc), 2 dc in same sp, ch 1; (sk next 3 dc, 3 dc in next ch-3 sp, ch 1) twice; * sk next 3 dc, 9 dc in next ch-5 corner sp, ch 1; (3 dc in next ch-3 sp, ch 1) 3 times; rep from * twice more; sk next 3 dc, 9 dc in next ch-5 corner sp, ch 1; join in 3rd ch of beg ch-3: 72 dc; finish off Color B.

Rnd 6: Join Color C in last ch-1 sp worked on prev rnd; ch 1, sc in same sp; * † [(sc between next 2 dc) twice, sc in next ch-1 sp] 3 times; (sc between next 2 dc) 8 times †, sc in next ch-1 sp; rep from * twice more, then rep from † to † once; join in first sc: 72 sc; finish off and weave in ends.

Chapter 2
GRANNY AFGHANS

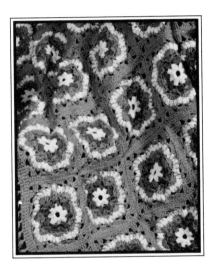

This collection of 16 beautiful afghans will keep you busy crocheting for a long time!

There's a wide variety of squares—from dimensional daffodils to octagons that form a quilt pattern.

Granny afghans make cherished family heirlooms, and wonderful gifts.

Granny's Rose Garden

DESIGNED BY JEAN LEINHAUSER

Size: About 43″ × 60″ before fringing

This lovely afghan reflects the love of flowers—especially big, full-blown roses—rampant in the Victorian days. This afghan is easy to make, as the dimensional roses are crocheted separately and then sewn to the granny squares.

Materials: Worsted weight yarn, 10½ oz dk pink; 17½ oz white; 22 oz lt gray; 16 oz black

Size J aluminum crochet hook, or size required for gauge

Gauge: 3 sc = 1″
   1 complete square = 8½″
   1 rose = 3¾″

INSTRUCTIONS

Granny square (make 35)

With white, ch 4, join with a sl st to form a ring.

Rnd 1: Ch 3, 2 dc in ring; (ch 2, 3 dc in ring) 3 times; ch 2, join with a sl st to top of beg ch-3.

Rnd 2: Sl st across next 2 dc and into ch-2 sp; ch 3, in same sp work (2 dc, ch 2, 3 dc); * in next ch-2 sp work (3 dc, ch 2, 3 dc); rep from * twice more; ch 2; join with a sl st in top of beg ch-3.

Rnd 3: Sl st across next 2 dc and into ch-2 sp; ch 3, in same sp work (2 dc, ch 2, 3 dc) for corner; * between next two 3-dc groups, work 3 dc for side; (3 dc, ch 2, 3 dc) for corner in next ch-2 sp; rep from * twice more; between next two 3-dc groups, work 3 dc for side; join with a sl st to top of beg ch-3.

Rnd 4: Sl st across next 2 dc and into ch-2 sp; † ch 3, in same sp work (dc, ch 2, 2 dc); * dc in next 9 dc, in next ch-2 sp work (2 dc, ch 2, 2 dc); rep from * 3 times more; dc in next 9 dc; join with a sl st to top of beg ch-3; finish off white.

Rnd 5: Join gray with a sl st in any ch-2 corner sp; work as for Rnd 4 from † around, working 13 dc between corner groups.

Rnd 6: Sl st across next dc and into ch-2 corner sp; * in same sp work 3 sc; sc in 17 dc along side; rep from * 3 times; sc in 17 dc; join to first sc of rnd with a sl st.

Rnd 7: Ch 1, 3 sc in next sc for corner; * sc in next 19 sc, 3 sc in next sc for corner; rep from * twice more; sc in next 19 sc; join with a sl st to beg ch-1 of rnd.

Rnd 8: Rep Rnd 7, working 21 sc between corners. Finish off gray.

Rnd 9: With black continue in same manner, working 23 sc between corners; join with a sl st to first ch-1, finish off. Weave in ends.

Rose (make 35)

With dk pink, ch 4, join with a sl st to form a ring.

Rnd 1: (Ch 4, sc in ring) 6 times: 6 ch-4 lps made.

Rnd 2: (In next lp, work petal of sc, hdc, 2 dc, hdc, sc) 6 times; join with a sl st between last lp and first lp of prev row: 6 petals made.

Rnd 3: * Ch 4, holding next petal forward and working behind it, sc in back lp of next sc made in Rnd 1; rep from * 5 times more: 6 ch-4 lps made; join with a sl st to joining sl st of Rnd 2.

Rnd 4: (In next ch-4 lp, work petal of sc, hdc, 3 dc, hdc, sc) 6 times: 6 petals made; join with a sl st in first sc of first petal; finish off, leaving a 10″ long yarn end for sewing later.

Finishing

Attaching Roses: Place a rose face up centered on the right side of a square. Thread long yarn end into tapestry needle, and firmly tack inner edge of outer row of petals to square; finish off yarn securely. Don't sew through outer edge of petals or you will lose the dimensional look.

Joining Squares: Join squares in rows of 5 squares wide by 7 squares long. To join squares, hold two squares with right sides tog; with black yarn, overcast loosely, working in back lps only (lp away from you) of each st, and carefully matching sts. Lightly steam seams (do not let iron rest on the afghan; let the steam do the work).

Edging: With right side of afghan facing you, join black in an outer corner; sc around, working 3 sc in center sc of each outer corner; join with a sl st, finish off.

Fringe

Following instructions for Single Knot Fringe on page 9, cut strands 17″ long and use 6 strands in each knot. Tie knots at outer corners and then in every third st across each short end of afghan.

Ruffled Gingham

DESIGNED BY JEAN LEINHAUSER

Size: About 40″ × 60″ before ruffle

Creamy, foamy ruffles make this afghan very special. Done in favorite Victorian shades of rose, this is fun to make.

Materials: Worsted weight yarn, 35 oz cream; 24 oz lt rose; 17 oz dk rose.

Size I aluminum crochet hook, or size required for gauge

Gauge: One Granny Square = 4″

INSTRUCTIONS

Granny Square Instructions

Ch 4, join with a sl st to form a ring.

Rnd 1: Ch 3 (counts as first dc), 2 dc in ring; * ch 2, 3 dc in ring; rep from * twice more; ch 2, join with a sl st in top of beg ch-3.

Rnd 2: Sl st in each of next 2 dc, sl st into ch-2 corner sp; ch 3, in same sp work (2 dc, ch 2, 3 dc); * in next corner sp work (3 dc, ch 2, 3 dc); rep from * twice more; join with a sl st in top of beg ch-3.

Rnd 3: Sl st in each of next 2 dc and into ch-2 corner sp; ch 3, in same sp work (2 dc, ch 2, 3 dc); * 3 dc in sp between next two 3-dc groups for side; in next corner sp work (3 dc, ch 2, 3 dc); rep from * twice more; 3 dc in sp between next two 3-dc groups; join with a sl st in top of beg ch-3; finish off and weave in ends.

Afghan Instructions

Following Granny Square Instructions, make 40 squares with dk rose, 75 squares with light rose and 35 squares with cream. Afghan has 15 rows with 10 squares in each row. Following color arrangement chart, join squares according to Joining Instructions.

Joining Instructions

Thread light rose yarn into tapestry needle. Holding 2 squares with right sides tog, join with overcast st in outer lps only. Work across each square, carefully matching sts. Join all squares in this manner whether joining squares for a row or joining rows of squares.

Edging

With right side facing you, join cream with a sl st in any corner sp of afghan, ch 1.

Rnd 1: Work 3 sc in same corner sp; sc in each dc across first square; * sc in next corner sp of same square, sc in corner sp of next square; sc in each dc across same square; rep from * around afghan; join with a sl st in first sc of rnd.

COLOR ARRANGEMENT CHART

D	L	D	L	D	L	D	L	D	L
L	C	L	C	L	C	L	C	L	C
D	L	D	L	D	L	D	L	D	L
L	C	L	C	L	C	L	C	L	C
D	L	D	L	D	L	D	L	D	L
L	C	L	C	L	C	L	C	L	C
D	L	D	L	D	L	D	L	D	L
L	C	L	C	L	C	L	C	L	C
D	L	D	L	D	L	D	L	D	L
L	C	L	C	L	C	L	C	L	C
D	L	D	L	D	L	D	L	D	L
L	C	L	C	L	C	L	C	L	C
D	L	D	L	D	L	D	L	D	L
L	C	L	C	L	C	L	C	L	C
D	L	D	L	D	L	D	L	D	L

D = Dark Rose   L = Light Rose   C = Cream

Rnd 2: Sl st in next sc, ch 5; dc in same sc, sk next sc; * in next sc work (dc, ch 2, dc), sk next sc; rep from * around; join with a sl st in third ch of beg ch-5.

Rnd 3: Sl st in first sp, ch 3; in same sp work (dc, ch 3, 2 dc); in each rem ch-2 sp work (2 dc, ch 3, 2 dc); join with a sl st in top of beg ch-3.

Rnd 4: Sl st in next dc and into ch-2 sp, ch 3; in same sp work (dc, ch 3, 2 dc); in each rem ch-2 sp work (2 dc, ch 3, 2 dc); join with a sl st in top of beg ch-3.

Rep Rnd 4 until ruffle measures 4″ wide.

Last Rnd: Sl st in next dc, sl st in ch-3 sp, ch 1; in same ch-3 sp work [hdc, dc; ch 4, sl st in 4th ch from hook (picot made); dc, hdc, sc, ch 1]; in each rem ch-3 sp work [sc, hdc, dc; ch 4, sl st in 4th ch from hook (picot made); dc, hdc, sc, ch 1]; at end, join with a sl st in beg ch-1; finish off and weave in ends.

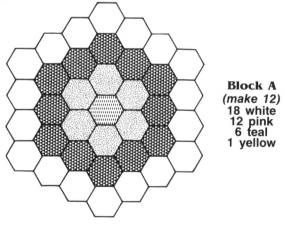

Grandmother's Flower Garden

DESIGNED BY JEAN LEINHAUSER

Size: About 52″ × 80″

This lovely afghan is adapted from a favorite old quilt pattern. Small hexagons are joined to make blocks, in the same way a quilt is made. We suggest making the hexagons for a few blocks then assembling these blocks. This way you won't get bored with making hexagons!

Materials: Worsted weight yarn, 32 oz off white; 32 oz dark pink; 18 oz light teal; 3½ oz yellow

Size H aluminum crochet hook, or size required for gauge

Gauge: 1 Hexagon = 2″ (flat side to flat side)

Note: The afghan is composed of hexagons which are joined into four different kinds of blocks. These blocks are then joined following a chart.

Basic Hexagon Pattern

Ch 5, join with a sl st to form a ring.

Rnd 1: Ch 3, 2 dc in ring; (ch 2, 3 dc in ring) 5 times; ch 2, join with sl st to top of beg ch-3; finish off, leaving a 12″ to 14″ yarn end for sewing later.

Joining

To join hexagons to form blocks, hold two hexagons tog with right sides facing; sew with overcast st, working in outer lps only, carefully matching sts. Whenever possible, use the 12″ to 14″ yarn end left for sewing.

INSTRUCTIONS

Block A (make 12)

Make 18 white, 12 pink, 6 teal and 1 yellow hexagon for each block. Join as shown in diagram; mark top of each block; set aside.

Block A
(make 12)
18 white
12 pink
6 teal
1 yellow

Color Key

= white = pink = teal = yellow

Block B (make 9)

Make 10 white, 12 pink, 6 teal and 1 yellow hexagon for each block. Join as shown in diagram; mark top of each block; set aside.

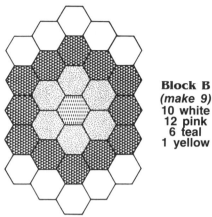

Block B
(make 9)
10 white
12 pink
6 teal
1 yellow

Block C (make 10)

Make 2 white, 12 pink, 6 teal and 1 yellow hexagon for each block. Join as shown in diagram; mark top of each block; set aside.

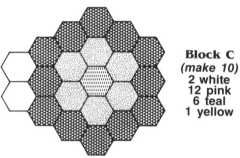

Block C
(make 10)
2 white
12 pink
6 teal
1 yellow

Block D (make 2)

Make 4 white, 12 pink, 6 teal and 1 yellow for each block. Join as shown in diagram; mark top of each block; set aside.

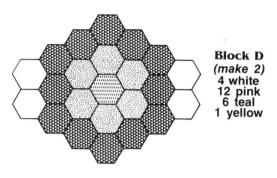

Block D
(make 2)
4 white
12 pink
6 teal
1 yellow

Joining Blocks

Using same sewing method as in joining hexagons, join blocks following **Fig 1**. Be sure all blocks are positioned correctly with marked tops at top. Work one rnd sc loosely around entire afghan. Lightly steam seams if needed.

Fig 1

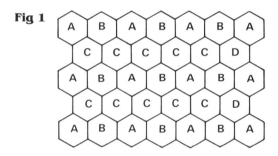

Sweet Memories

DESIGNED BY JEAN LEINHAUSER

Size: About 45″ × 59″

This is a new, fun-to-do granny square design that will be perfectly at home in any decor. We have shown it in country colors for a traditional granny square design.

Materials: Worsted weight yarn, 19 oz tan; 21 oz blue; 9 oz dk rose

Size J aluminum crochet hook, or size required for gauge

Gauge: 4 sc = 1″
          One square = 7″

INSTRUCTIONS

Square instructions (make 48)

With blue, ch 2.

Rnd 1: 4 sc in 2nd ch from hook. Do not join and do not turn; work in spiral, marking beg of rnds.

Rnd 2: (3 sc in next sc) 4 times: 12 sc.

Rnd 3: (3 sc in next sc, sc in next 2 sc) 4 times: 4 corners with 2 sc between.

Rnd 4: Sc in next sc; (3 sc in next sc, sc in next 4 sc) 3 times; 3 sc in next sc, sc in next 3 sc.

Rnd 5: Sc in next 2 sc; (3 sc in next sc, sc in next 6 sc) 3 times; 3 sc in next sc, sc in next 4 sc.

Rnd 6: Sc in next 3 sc; (3 sc in next sc, sc in next 8 sc) 3 times; 3 sc in next sc, sc in next 5 sc.

Rnd 7: Sc in next 4 sc; (3 sc in next sc, sc in next 10 sc) 3 times; 3 sc in next sc, sc in next 6 sc.

Rnd 8: Sc in next 5 sc, draw lp of tan yarn through last sc, drop blue; (3 sc in next sc, sc in next 12 sc) 3 times; 3 sc in next sc, sc in next 12 sc, working through marked beg st of rnd to corner; finish off tan and cut blue yarn.

Rnd 9: Join dk rose with a sl st in center sc of any corner; ch 3 (counts as dc), in same sc work (dc, ch 2, 2 dc): corner made; * † ch 1, (sk 2 sc, 2 dc in next sc, ch 1) 4 times †; sk 2 sc, in next sc work (2 dc, ch 2, 2 dc): corner made; rep from * twice more, then rep from † to † once; sk 2 sc; join with a sl st in 3rd ch of beg ch-3; finish off dk rose.

Rnd 10: Join tan with a sl st in any ch-2 corner sp; ch 1, 3 sc in same sp: corner made; * (sc in next 2 dc, sc in ch-1 sp) 5 times; sc in next 2 dc, 3 sc in next ch-2 sp: corner made; rep from * 3 times more, ending last rep without working last 3 sc: 17 sc between corners; sc in next sc.

Rnd 11: (3 sc in next sc, sc in next 19 sc) 4 times: 19 sc between corners; sc in next sc, sl st in next sc; finish off and weave in ends.

Assembling

Join squares in 8 rows of 6 squares. To join squares, hold two squares with right sides tog. Carefully matching sts on both squares and with tan, sew with overcast st in bls only (see page 10) across side, beg and ending with one corner st. Join squares in rows; then sew rows tog in same manner, being sure that all four-corner junctions are firmly joined.

Edging

Holding afghan with right side facing you, join blue with a sl st in center sc of 3-sc corner group of upper right-hand outer corner.

Rnd 1: Ch 1, 3 sc in same sc: corner made; * sc in each sc and in each joining across side; 3 sc in center sc of next 3-sc corner group; rep from * twice more; sc in each sc and in each joining across last side; join with a sl st in beg ch-1.

Rnd 2: Sc in next sc, 3 sc in next sc: corner made; sc in each sc around, working 3 sc in center sc of each 3-sc corner group; join with a sl st in beg sc; finish off blue.

Rnd 3: Join dk rose with a sl st in center sc of any 3-sc outer corner group; ch 3, in same sc work (dc, ch 2, 2 dc): corner made; [* ch 1, sk 2 sc, 2 dc in next sc; rep from * to next corner, adjusting sts as you work so that you can sk 2 sc before center sc of next 3-sc corner group; in center sc of next 3-sc corner group, work (2 dc, ch 2, 2 dc)] 4 times, omitting last (2 dc, ch 2, 2 dc) on last rep; join with a sl st in 3rd ch of beg ch-3; finish off dk rose.

Rnd 4: Join blue with a sl st in ch-2 sp of any corner; ch 1, 3 sc in same sp; * sc in each sc and in each ch-1 sp across side, 3 sc in next ch-2 sp; rep from * around; join with a sl st in beg ch-1.

Rnd 5: Sl st in next sc, sc in next sc; * sk 2 sc, 5 dc in next sc: shell made; sk 2 sc, sc in next sc; rep from * around; join with a sl st in beg ch-1; finish off and weave in ends.

Traditional Granny

DESIGNED BY ELEANOR DENNER

Size: 45″ × 63″ before fringing

Materials: Worsted weight yarn, 13 oz black; 24 oz raspberry; 11 oz med blue

Size I aluminum crochet hook, or size required for gauge

Gauge: One square = 9″

INSTRUCTIONS

Granny Square *(make 35)*

With black, ch 4, join to form a ring.

Rnd 1: Ch 3 (counts as a dc in this and all following rnds), 2 dc in ring; (ch 3, 3 dc in ring) 3 times; ch 3; join in 3rd ch of beg ch-3: 4 ch-3 sps; finish off.

Rnd 2: Join med blue in any ch-3 sp, ch 6 (counts as a dc and ch 3), dc in same sp: corner made; dc in next 3 dc; * in next ch-3 sp work (dc, ch 3, dc): corner made; dc in next 3 dc; rep from * twice more; join in 3rd ch of beg ch-6: 5 dc between ch-3 corner sps.

Rnd 3: Sl st in ch-3 corner sp, ch 3 (counts as a dc), in same sp work (2 dc, ch 3, 3 dc): corner made; * sk 2 dc, 3 dc in next dc, sk 2 dc; in next ch-3 corner sp work (3 dc, ch 3, 3 dc); rep from * twice more; sk 2 dc, 3 dc in next dc, sk 2 dc, join in 3rd ch of beg ch-3: 9 dc between corner sps.

Rnd 4: Sl st in next 2 dc and ch-3 corner sp; ch 6 (counts as a dc and ch 3), dc in same sp: corner made; dc in next 9 dc; * in next ch-3 corner sp work (dc, ch 3, dc): corner made; dc in next 9 dc; rep from * twice more; join in 3rd ch of beg ch-6: 11 dc between corner sps; finish off.

Rnd 5: Join dk rose with a sl st in any ch-3 corner sp; ch 3 (counts as a dc), in same sp work (2 dc, ch 3, 3 dc): corner made; * (sk 2 dc, 3 dc in next dc) 3 times; sk next 2 dc, in next ch-3 corner sp work (3 dc, ch 3, 3 dc); rep from * twice more; (sk next 2 dc, 3 dc in next dc) 3 times, sk next 2 dc; join in 3rd ch of beg ch-3: 15 dc between corner sps.

Rnd 6: Sl st in next 2 dc and ch-3 corner sp; ch 6 (counts as a dc and ch-3 sp), dc in same sp: corner made; dc in next 15 sc; * in next ch-3 corner sp work (dc, ch 3, dc): corner made; dc in next 15 dc; rep from * twice more; join in 3rd ch of beg ch-6: 17 dc between corner sps.

Rnd 7: Sl st in ch-3 sp; ch 3 (counts as a dc), in same sp work (2 dc, ch 3, 3 dc): corner made; * (sk next 2 dc, 3 dc in next dc) 5 times; sk 2 dc, in next ch-3 corner sp work (3 dc, ch 3, 3 dc); rep from * twice more; (sk next 2 dc, 3 dc in next dc) 5 times, sk next 2 dc; join in 3rd ch of beg ch-3: 21 dc between corner sps; finish off.

Rnd 8: Join black in any ch-3 corner sp; ch 3 (counts as a dc), 4 dc in same sp; * dc in next 21 dc, 5 dc in next ch-3 corner sp; rep from * twice more; dc in next 21 dc; join in 3rd ch of beg ch-3; finish off and weave in ends.

Joining

Join squares in 7 rows of 5 squares. To join squares, hold two squares with right sides tog. Carefully matching sts on both squares and with black, sew with overcast st in bls only (see page 10) across side, beg and ending with one corner st. Join squares in rows; then sew rows tog in same manner, being sure that all four-corner junctions are firmly joined.

Edging

With right side of afghan facing you, join black in center dc of upper right-hand corner.

Rnd 1: Ch 1, 3 sc in same dc as joining, sc in each dc around, working 3 sc in center dc of each rem outer corner; join in first sc.

Fringe

Following Fringe instructions on page 9, make single knot fringe. Cut 16″ strands; use 6 strands, 2 of each color, for each knot. Tie knots in every 3rd st across each short end of afghan. Trim ends evenly.

Granny's Daffodils

DESIGNED BY MARY ANN SIPES

Size: About 67″ in diameter

This unique hexagon was inspired by the designer's memories of her grandmother's daffodil patch. Wouldn't it be delightful to keep warm on a cold winter's night with this reminder of Spring?

Materials: Worsted weight yarn, 20 oz yellow; 37 oz medium green; 29 oz dk green

Size J aluminum crochet hook and size H aluminum crochet hook, or sizes required for gauge

Gauge: With size J hook, 3 dc = 1″
One hexagon = 7½″

Stitch Note: CLUSTER. YO, insert hook from front to back to front around post of next st and pull up a lp; YO and draw through 2 lps on hook; YO, insert hook around post of same st and pull up a lp; YO and draw through 2 lps on hook; YO and draw through 3 lps on hook: cluster made.

INSTRUCTIONS

Hexagon *(make 37 medium green and 24 dk green)*

Flower stem

Note: Flower stem is worked from bottom to top for first 3 rnds. Rnd 4 completes top edge of stem; sl sts are then used to return yarn to bottom of stem.

With smaller size hook and with yellow, ch 4; join with a sl st to form a ring.

Rnd 1: Ch 1, 6 sc in ring: 6 sc; join with a sl st in beg ch-1.

Rnd 2: Ch 1, sc in each sc; join with a sl st in beg ch-1.

Rnd 3: Rep Rnd 2.

Rnd 4: Ch 3, sl st in bl of next sc; (sk next sc, sl st in bl of next sc, ch 3, sl st in same sc) twice; join with a sl st in joining sl st. Turning stem sideways, sl st in each prev sc rnd; sl st in unused lp of Rnd 1; ch 1, turn.

Flower center

Note: Flower center is worked from bottom to top and in opposite direction from bottom of stem (**Fig 1**).

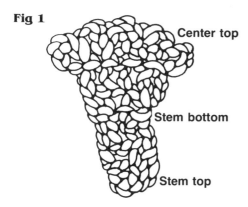

Fig 1

Center top

Stem bottom

Stem top

Rnd 1: With bottom of stem facing you, sc in each unused lp of Rnd 1 of stem: 6 sc; join with a sl st in beg ch-1.

Rnd 2: Ch 1, (sc in bl of next sc, 2 sc in bl of next sc) 3 times: 9 sc; join with a sl st in beg sc.

Rnd 3: Ch 3 (counts as dc), dc in each sc: 9 dc; join with a sl st in 3rd ch of beg ch-3.

Rnd 4: (Ch 3, sl st in bl of next dc) 8 times; join with a sl st in joining sl st: 8 ch-3 lps; finish off and weave in ends. Turn Flower center up around stem.

Flower base and Petals

With right side of flower facing you and with larger size hook, join yellow in unused lp of Rnd 1 of stem.

Rnd 1: Ch 1, (2 sc in next unused lp) 6 times: 12 sc; join with a sl st in beg sc.

Rnd 2: * In next sc work (sc, dc, trc; ch 1, sl st through top 2 lps of trc just made; trc, dc, sc); sl st in next sc: petal made; rep from * 5 times more: 6 petals made; join with a sl st in joining sl st.

Rnd 3: Working each ch-3 behind Petals, (ch 3, sl st in sl st between next 2 Petals) 6 times: 6 ch-3 lps; finish off yellow.

Leaves

With right side of flower facing you and with larger size hook, join medium green (or dk green) with a sl st in sl st between any 2 Petals.

Rnd 1: Ch 4 (counts as a trc), * 3 trc in next ch-3 sp, sl st in lp directly behind ch-1 at top of next Petal; 3 trc in same ch-3 sp; trc in sl st between next 2 Petals; rep from * 5 times more, ending last rep without working last trc; join with a sl st in 4th ch of beg ch-4.

Rnd 2: Ch 3 (counts as a dc in this and all following rnds), 2 dc in same st as joining, work cluster around post of next trc, hdc in next 5 trc; * work cluster around post of next trc, 3 dc in next trc, work cluster around post of next trc, hdc in next 5 trc; rep from * 4 times more; work cluster around post of next trc; join with a sl st in 3rd ch of beg ch-3.

Rnd 3: Sl st in next dc, ch 3, sk next dc, work cluster around next cluster; * hdc in next 5 hdc, 2 hdc in top st of next cluster; work cluster around same cluster, sk next dc, dc in next dc, sk next dc, work cluster around next cluster; rep from * 4 times more; hdc in next 5 hdc, 2 hdc in top st of next cluster, work cluster around same cluster, sk next dc; join with a sl st in 3rd ch of beg ch-3.

Rnd 4: Sl st in top st of next cluster and in next hdc, ch 2 (counts as a hdc in this rnd and following rnd), hdc in next 6 hdc, ch 1; * † work cluster around next cluster, holding last 3 lps on hook, sk next dc, work cluster around next cluster,

holding last 2 lps on hook; YO and draw through 5 lps on hook; ch 1 †, hdc in next 7 hdc, ch 1; rep from * 4 times more, then rep from † to † once; join with a sl st in 2nd ch of beg ch-2.

Rnd 5: Ch 2, hdc in next 6 hdc, hdc in next ch 1; * in top of next cluster work (2 hdc, ch 1, 2 hdc): corner made; hdc in next ch 1, hdc in next 7 hdc, hdc in next ch 1; rep from * 4 times more; in top of next cluster work (2 hdc, ch 1, 2 hdc): corner made; ch 1; join with a sl st in 2nd ch of beg ch-2. Finish off green and weave in ends.

Finishing

Note: Hexagons are joined with a crochet hook using a zig-zag sl st method. When joining hexagons, hold yarn beneath work on wrong side. Insert hook from right to wrong side and draw yarn up from beneath work. Do not work tightly.

To join, place 2 hexagons side by side with right sides facing you. Join yarn as specified in each row with a sl st in ch-1 corner of joining edge of first hexagon; ch 1, sl st in same ch 1, sl st in corresponding ch 1 of second hexagon, sl st in next hdc of first hexagon, then sl st in corresponding st of 2nd hexagon. Continue across joining edges.

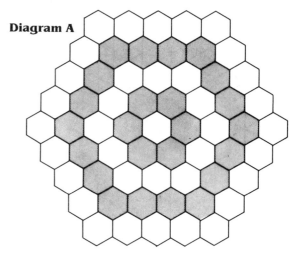

Diagram A

Referring to Diagram A, join hexagons as follows, beg with one medium green hexagon as center of afghan.

Row 1: With larger size hook and dk green, join 6 dk green hexagons to center hexagon and to each other.

Row 2: With dk green, join 12 medium green hexagons to prev row of hexagons. Join sides with medium green.

Row 3: With dk green, join 18 dk green hexagons to prev row of hexagons and to each other.

Row 4: With dk green, join 24 medium green hexagons to prev row of hexagons. Join sides with medium green.

Border

With right side of afghan facing you and with larger size hook, join dk green with a sl st in ch 1 of outer corner of any hexagon.

Row 1: Ch 1, sl st in lp directly behind ch 1 just worked (**Fig 2**); * sl st in next st, ch 1, sl st in lp directly behind ch 1 just worked, ch 1; rep from * around afghan; join with a sl st in joining sl st; finish off and weave in ends.

Fig 2

Basket Quilt
DESIGNED BY RITA WEISS

Size: About 55″ × 70″

This breathtaking afghan is an adaptation of a 1930's quilt pattern in Rita's collection. It would look beautifully at home in a country or modern room setting. Although it is time-consuming to make, it is well worth every minute!

Materials: Worsted weight yarn, 46 oz eggshell; 36 oz pink
Size G aluminum crochet hook, or size required for gauge

Gauge: One square = 2½″
One block = 15″

INSTRUCTIONS

Block instructions (make 12)

One-color square (make 20)

With eggshell, ch 4, join with a sl st to form a ring.

Rnd 1 (wrong side): Ch 3, (counts as a dc in this and following rnd), 2 dc in ring; (ch 2, 3 dc in ring) 3 times, ch 2; join with a sl st in 3rd ch of beg ch-3, turn.

Rnd 2: Sk joining st, sl st in next ch st and into ch-2 sp; ch 3, 2 dc in same sp; * ch 1, in next ch-2 sp work (3 dc, ch 2, 3 dc): corner made; rep from * twice more; ch 1, 3 dc in beg ch-2 sp, ch 2; join with a sl st in 3rd ch of beg ch-3; finish off and weave in ends.

Diagonal two-color square (make 16)

With eggshell, ch 4, join with a sl st to form a ring.

Rnd 1 (wrong side): Ch 3 (counts as a dc in this and following rnd), 2 dc in ring; ch 2, 3 dc in ring; drop eggshell, but do not cut yarn; with pink, ch 2 (**Fig 1**), continuing with pink, (3 dc in ring, ch 2) twice; join with a sl st in 3rd ch of beg eggshell ch-3, turn.

Fig 1

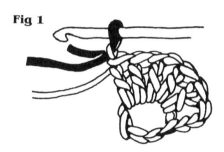

Rnd 2: Sk joining st, sl st in next ch st and into ch-2 sp; ch 3, 2 dc in same sp; ch 1, in next ch-2 sp work (3 dc, ch 2, 3 dc): corner made; ch 1, 3 dc in next ch-2 sp, ch 2; drop pink; loosely drawing up eggshell, work 3 dc in same ch-2 sp, ch 1; continuing with eggshell, in next ch-2 sp work (3 dc, ch 2, 3 dc), ch 1, 3 dc in beg ch-2 sp, ch 2; join with a sl st in 3rd ch of beg pink ch-3; finish off eggshell. Cut pink and weave in all ends.

Assembling block

Arrange squares as shown in **Fig 2**. To join squares, hold two squares with right sides tog. Carefully matching sts on both squares and with eggshell, sew with overcast st in bls only (see page 10) across side, beg and ending with one corner st. Join squares in rows; then sew rows tog in same manner, being sure that all four corner junctions are firmly joined.

Fig 2

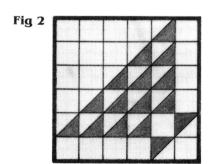

Basket handles (make 12)

With pink, ch 3.

Row 1: Sc in 2nd ch from hook and in next ch: 2 sc; ch 1, turn.

Row 2: Sc in each sc; ch 1, turn.

Rep Row 2 until handle measures about 17″ long. Finish off and weave in all ends.

With matching yarn, sew in place on each square as shown in **Fig 3**.

Fig 3

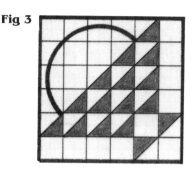

Joining

Join blocks as shown in **Fig 4**, in same manner as squares were joined.

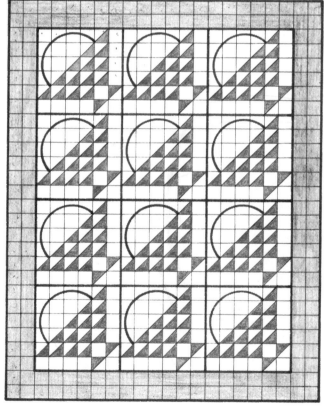

Fig 4

Border

With pink, make 184 one-color squares. Referring to **Fig 4** for placement and with pink, join squares to quilt in same manner as squares and blocks were joined. Weave in all ends.

Snow White Granny

DESIGNED BY MARY ANN FRITS

Size: About 45″ × 67″ before fringing

Imagine sitting by the television watching your favorite classic movie video and eating popcorn. Now add this classic all-white afghan to keep your toes warm and the picture is complete!

Materials: Worsted weight yarn, 76 oz white
Size H aluminum crochet hook, or size required for gauge

Gauge: 4 dc = 1″
One square = 7½″

Stitch Note: POPCORN (PC). Work 5 dc in st or ring; drop lp from hook, insert hook in first dc made and draw dropped lp through st on hook: PC made.

INSTRUCTIONS

Square (make 54)

Ch 6, join with a sl st to form a ring.

Rnd 1: Ch 3 (counts as a dc in this and all following rnds), dc in ring, PC in ring, 2 dc in ring; * ch 2, in ring work (2 dc, PC, 2 dc); rep from * twice more; ch 2; join with a sl st in 3rd ch of beg ch-3.

Rnd 2: Ch 3, dc in next dc, dc in st behind PC, dc in next 2 dc; * in next ch-2 sp work (dc, ch 3, dc): corner made; dc in next 2 dc, dc in st behind next PC, dc in next 2 dc; rep from * twice more; in next ch-2 sp work (dc, ch 3, dc): corner made; join with a sl st in 3rd ch of beg ch-3.

Rnd 3: Ch 3, PC in next dc, dc in next dc, PC in next dc, dc in next 2 dc; * in next ch-3 corner sp work (dc, ch 3, dc): corner made; dc in next 2 dc, PC in next dc, dc in next dc, PC in next dc, dc in next 2 dc; rep from * twice more; in next ch-3 corner sp work (dc, ch 3, dc): corner made; dc in next dc; join with a sl st in 3rd ch of beg ch-3.

Rnd 4: Ch 3, * † dc in st behind next PC, dc in next dc, dc in st behind next PC, dc in next 3 dc; in next ch-3 corner sp work (dc, ch 4, dc): corner made †; dc in next 3 dc; rep from * twice more, then rep from † to † once; dc in next 2 dc; join with a sl st in 3rd ch of beg ch-3.

Rnd 5: Sl st in next dc, ch 3, * PC in next dc, dc in next dc, PC in next dc, dc in next 3 dc; in next ch-4 corner sp work (dc, ch 4, dc): corner made; dc in next 3 dc, PC in next dc, dc in next dc; rep from * 3 times more, ending last rep without working last dc; join with a sl st in 3rd ch of beg ch-3.

Rnd 6: Ch 3, * dc in st behind next PC, dc in next dc, dc in st behind next PC, dc in next 4 dc; in next ch-4 corner sp work (dc, ch 5, dc): corner made; dc in next 4 dc, dc in st behind next PC, dc in next dc; rep from * 3 times more, ending last rep without working last dc; join with a sl st in 3rd ch of beg ch-3.

Rnd 7: Ch 3, dc in next 8 dc; * in next ch-5 corner sp work (3 dc, trc, 3 dc): corner made; dc in next 15 dc; rep from * twice more; in next ch-5 corner space work (3 dc, trc, 3 dc): corner made; dc in next 6 dc; join with a sl st in 3rd ch of beg ch-3; finish off.

Assembling

Join squares in 9 rows of 6 squares. To join squares, hold two squares with right sides tog. Carefully matching sts on both squares, sew with overcast st in bls only (see page 10) across side, beg and ending with one corner st. Join squares in rows; then sew rows tog in same manner, being sure that all four-corner junctions are firmly joined.

Border

With right side of afghan facing you, join yarn with a sl st in trc of upper right-hand outer corner.

Row 1: Ch 1, in same trc work (dc, sc); * † sc in each st across square to last st before joining; hdc in next st, dc in joining, hdc in next st †; rep from † to † 4 times more; sc in each st across square to trc in next outer corner; in trc work (sc, dc, sc); rep from † to † 8 times; sc in each st across square to trc in next outer corner; in trc work (sc, dc, sc); rep from * once more, omitting last (sc, dc, sc); join with a sl st in beg ch-1.

Row 2: Ch 1, 3 sc in next dc, sc in each st around afghan, working 3 sc in each dc of each rem outer corner; join with a sl st in beg ch-1; finish off and weave in ends.

Fringe

Following Fringe instructions on page 9, make single knot fringe. Cut 20″ strands; use 6 strands for each knot. Tie knots evenly spaced (about every 3rd st) across each short end of afghan. Trim ends evenly.

Rose in Bloom

Size: About 47″ × 62″

Beautiful cabbage roses bloom happily on this pretty afghan, which makes a warm and romantic cover.

Materials: Coats & Clark Red Heart "Premier 4-Ply Yarn", 32 oz Off White; 30 oz Dusty Rose; 14 oz Teal
Size I aluminum crochet hook, or size required for gauge

Gauge: One square = 7½″

INSTRUCTIONS

Rose Square (make 48)

With dusty rose, ch 6, join to form a ring.

Rnd 1: (Sc in ring, ch 5) 8 times; do not join.

Rnd 2: In each ch-5 lp work (sc, hdc, dc, hdc, sc) for petal: 8 petals made.

Rnd 3: Holding next petal forward, sc in back of first sc of Rnd 1, ch 4; * sc in back of next sc of Rnd 1 between petals, ch 4; rep from * 6 times more: 8 ch-4 lps.

Rnd 4: In each ch-4 lp work (sc, hdc, 3 dc, hdc, sc) for petal: 8 petals made.

Rnd 5: Holding next petal forward, sc in back of first sc of Rnd 3, ch 4; * sc in back of next sc of Rnd 3 between petals, ch 4; rep from * 6 times more: 8 ch-4 lps.

Rnd 6: In each ch-4 lp work (sc, hdc, 5 dc, hdc, sc) for petal; join to first sc; finish off.

Note: Following rnds use double triple crochet, abbreviated dtrc. To work dtrc: YO hook 3 times, YO and pull through 2 lps four times: dtrc made.

Rnd 7: Join teal to center dc of any petal of Rnd 6; ch 3 (counts as a dc), holding back last lp of each dc on hook, 2 dc in same dc, YO and draw through all 3 lps on hook: 2-dc cluster made; ch 2, holding back last lp of each dc on hook, 3 dc in same dc, YO and draw through all 4 lps on hook: 3-dc cluster made; * ch 3, in center dc of next petal, work corner group as follows: holding back last lp of each trc on hook, 3 trc in dc, YO and draw through all 4 lps on hook: 3-trc cluster made; ch 4; in same dc, in same manner work 3-dtrc cluster, ch 4, 3-trc cluster; ch 3, in center of dc of next petal work (3-dc cluster, ch 2, 3-dc cluster); rep from * twice more; work corner group; ch 3; join in top of first cluster; finish off.

Rnd 8: Join off white in top of center dtrc cluster of any corner group; ch 3, 2 dc in same place; (3 dc in next sp) 5 times; * in top of next dtrc cluster work (3 dc, ch 3, 3 dc): corner made; (3 dc in next sp) 5 times; rep from * twice more; 3 dc in next sp, ch 3; join in 3rd ch of beg ch-3.

Rnd 9: Ch 3, * dc in each dc to corner; in next ch-3 corner sp work (3 dc, ch 3, 3 dc); rep from * around; join in 3rd ch of beg ch-3; finish off and weave in ends.

Assembling

Join squares in 6 rows of 8 squares each. To join, hold squares with right sides tog and overcast loosely through bls only, carefully matching sts.

Edging

Hold afghan with right side of afghan facing you; join off white in any outer ch-3 corner sp; ch 3 (counts as a dc), in same sp work (2 dc, ch 3, 3 dc): corner made; * dc in each dc to next outer ch-3 corner sp; in ch-3 corner sp work (3 dc, ch 3, 3 dc): corner made; rep from * twice more; dc in each dc to first corner; join in 3rd ch of beg ch-3; finish off and weave in ends.

(*left*) Snow White Granny, p. 30; (*right*) Delft Tiles, p. 60

(*left*) Pretty in Pink Cardigan, p. 84;
(*right*) Flower Petals Vest, p. 88

Log Cabin Placemat and Napkin, p. 114

(*left*) Puff Sleeve Sweater, p. 86; (*right*) Sleeveless Shell Top, p. 90

Log Cabin and Granny's Ring Slippers, p. 138

Shades of Purple Placemat, p. 118

Sunflower Tote, p.141

Accent Potholders, p.110

Chrysanthemum Table Runner, p.124

Hostess Apron, p.100

35

Granny Scarf, p.132

Blue Jumper and Shawl, p.62

Rose Bouquet Bedspread, p.52

Wagon Wheel Pillow, p.111

Granny's Baby Layette, p. 76

Field of Flowers Baby Afghan, p. 79

Petal Rose Afghan and Pillow, p. 54

Granny's Daffodils, p.26

Grape Fizz, p. 49

Warm-up Lounging Robe, p. 104

Sweet Child Jacket, Bonnet and Afghan, p. 80

Pillow of Pinks, p. 113

Sunflower Sun Top, p. 92

Sunflower Bikini and Beach Skirt, p. 93

Sunflower Bikini, p. 93

(*left*) Basket Quilt, p. 28; (*right*) Rose Garden, p. 50

Rainbow Vest, p. 68

Blue Rhapsody Placemat and Tea Cozy, p. 108

Granny's Rose Garden, p.16

Shoulder Bag and Hat, p.126

Pretty Punkin Baby Afghan, Cardigan and Bonnet, p.65

Starburst Pin Cushion, p. 117

Sunburst Jumper, p. 70

Color Blocks Scarf, Hat and Bag, p. 134

Rose in Bloom, p. 32

(*left*) Diagonal Diamonds Granny, p. 56; (*middle*) Sweet Memories, p. 22; (*right*) Country Granny, p. 58

Pink Potholders, p. 123

Wagon Wheel Pullover, p. 103

Strawberries and Cream Placemat, p. 112

Crocheted Towel, p. 116

Grandmother's Flower Garden, p. 20

Traditional Granny, p. 24

46

Ruffled Gingham, p. 18

Granny Pullover, p. 73

Granny Shawl, p. 133

Shopping Bag, p. 129

Rainbow Granny Jacket, p. 97

Circle-In-A-Square Shawl, p. 130

Colorful Towels, p. 120

Best Friend's Coat, p. 136

Grape Fizz
DESIGNED BY ELEANOR DENNER

Size: About 50″ × 63″ before fringing

Materials: Worsted weight yarn, 54 oz purple
Size J aluminum crochet hook, or size required for gauge

Gauge: 4 dc = 1″
One 10-rnd square = 12½″

INSTRUCTIONS

Granny square (make 20)

Ch 4, join with a sl st to form a ring.

Rnd 1: Ch 3 (counts as a dc in this and all following rnds), 2 dc in ring; (ch 3, 3 dc in ring) 3 times; ch 3; join with a sl st in 3rd ch of beg ch-3.

Rnd 2: Sl st in next 2 dc and into ch-3 sp; ch 3, in same sp work (dc, ch 3, 2 dc): corner made; * dc in next 3 dc, in next ch-3 sp work (2 dc, ch 3, 2 dc): corner made; rep from * twice more; dc in next 3 dc; join with a sl st in 3rd ch of beg ch-3.

Rnd 3: Sl st in next dc and into next ch-3 corner sp; ch 3, in same sp work (dc, ch 3, 2 dc): corner made; * dc in next 3 dc, ch 1, sk next dc, dc in next 3 dc, in next ch-3 corner sp work (2 dc, ch 3, 2 dc): corner made; rep from * twice more; dc in next 3 dc, ch 1, sk next dc, dc in next 3 dc; join with a sl st in 3rd ch of beg ch-3.

Rnd 4: Sl st in next dc and into next ch-3 corner sp; ch 3, in same sp work (dc, ch 3, 2 dc): corner made; * † dc in next 3 dc, ch 1, sk next dc, dc in next dc, ch 1, sk next ch-1, dc in next dc, ch 1, sk next dc, dc in next 3 dc †, in next ch-3 corner sp work (2 dc, ch 3, 2 dc): corner made; rep from * twice more, then rep from † to † once; join with a sl st in 3rd ch of beg ch-3: 3 ch-1 sps between corners.

Rnd 5: Sl st in next dc and into ch-3 corner sp; ch 3, in same sp work (dc, ch 3, 2 dc): corner made; * † dc in next 3 dc, ch 1, sk next dc, (dc in next dc, ch 1, sk next ch-1) 4 times, dc in next 3 dc †, in next ch-3 corner sp work (2 dc, ch 3, 2 dc): corner made; rep from * twice more, then rep from † to † once; join with a sl st in 3rd ch of beg ch-3: 5 ch-1 sps between corner.

Rnds 6 through 10: Rep Rnd 5, increasing the number of ch-1 sps on each side in each successive rnd by 2; Rnd 10: 15 ch-1 sps. Finish off and weave in ends.

Assembling

Join squares in 5 rows of 4 squares. To join, hold two squares with right sides tog. Carefully matching sts on both squares, sew with overcast sts in bls only (see page 10) across side, beg and ending with one corner st. Join squares in rows, then sew rows tog in same manner, being sure that all four-corner junctions are firmly joined.

Fringe

Following Fringe instructions on page 9, make triple knot fringe. Cut 30″ strands; use 6 strands for each knot of fringe. Tie knots evenly spaced (about every 3rd st) across each short end of afghan. Then work double and triple knots per instructions. Trim ends evenly.

Rose Garden

DESIGNED BY JEAN LEINHAUSER

Size: About 45″ × 63″ before fringing

Everything will surely be coming up roses with this colorful afghan cuddled around you! Use the same colors as our model afghan, or choose your own favorite color scheme.

Materials: Worsted weight yarn, 16 oz eggshell; 43 oz dk pink; 7 oz dk rose; 6 oz jade green

Size I aluminum crochet hook, or size required for gauge

Gauge: 3 dc = 1″

One square = 9″

INSTRUCTIONS

Square (make 35)

With eggshell, ch 6, join with a sl st to form a ring.

Rnd 1: Ch 3 (counts as a dc in this and all following rnds), 2 dc in ring; (ch 1, 3 dc in ring) 7 times, ch 1; join with sl st in 3rd ch of beg ch-3: 8, 3-dc groups. Finish off eggshell.

Rnd 2: Join dk rose with sl st in any ch-1 sp; ch 3, 5 dc in same sp; (6 dc in next ch-1 sp) 7 times; join with sl st in 3rd ch of beg ch-3: 8, 6-dc groups. Finish off dk rose.

Rnd 3: Join jade with sl st between any two 6-dc groups; in same sp work shell of (sc, dc, sc, dc, sc); * ch 2, between next two 6-dc groups work shell of (sc, dc, sc, dc, sc); rep from * 6 times more; ch 2; join with sl st in beg sc; finish off jade.

Rnd 4: Join dk pink in first dc of any shell; ch 3, 5 dc in same dc: shell made; * sc in next ch-2 sp, in next dc work shell of 6 dc; rep from * 6 times more; sc in next ch-2 sp; join with sl st in 3rd ch of beg ch-3: 8 shells. Finish off dk pink.

Rnd 5: Join eggshell in first dc of any shell; in same dc work (ch 3, dc); work 2 dc in each of next 5 dc of shell: 12-dc scallop made; * 2 dc in each of next 6 dc: 12-dc scallop made; rep from * 6 times more; join with sl st in 3rd ch of beg ch-3: 8 scallops. Finish off eggshell.

Rnd 6: Join dk pink between center two 2-dc groups of any scallop; sc in same sp; (ch 2, sc between next two 2-dc groups) twice; * ch 2, sk sp between next two 2-dc groups, sc in next sp; (ch 2, sc in next sp) 4 times; rep from * 6 times more; ch 2, sk sp between next two 2-dc groups; (sc in next sp, ch 2) twice; join with sl st in beg sc.

Rnd 7: In same sc as joining, work (ch 4, 2 trc, ch 3, 3 trc): corner made; * ch 1, sk next 2 ch-2 sps, 5 dc in next ch-2 sp; ch 1, sk next 2 sc, 3 sc in next sc; ch 1, sk next 2 ch-2 sps, 5 dc in next ch-2 sp; ch 1, sk 2 sc, in next sc work (3 trc, ch 3, 3 trc): corner made; rep from * 3 times more, ending last rep without working corner; join with sl st in 4th ch of beg ch-4.

Rnd 8: Working loosely, sc in same ch as joining; sc in next 2 trc, 3 sc in ch-3 sp, sc in next 3 trc; sc in each st around (do not sc in ch-1 sps), working 3 sc in each ch-3 corner sp; join with sl st in beg sc; finish off and weave in ends.

Assembling

Join squares in 7 rows of 5 squares. To join squares, hold two squares with right sides tog. Carefully matching sts on both squares, sew with overcast st in bls only (see page 10) across side, beg and ending with one corner st. Join squares in rows; then sew rows tog in same manner, being sure that all four-corner junctions are firmly joined.

Border

With right side of afghan facing you, join yarn with a sl st in center sc of upper right-hand outer corner.

Row 1: Ch 1, sc in same sc as joining; * (sc in next 21 sc, hdc in next sc, dc in joining, hdc in next sc) 4 times; sc in next 21 sc, 3 sc in next sc: corner made; (sc in next 21 sc, hdc in next sc, dc in joining, hdc in next sc) 6 times; sc in next 21 sc, 3 sc in next sc: corner made; rep from * once more, omitting last 3 sc; join with a sl st in beg ch-1.

Row 2: Ch 1, 2 sc in same st as joining, sc in each sc around afghan, working 3 sc in center sc of each rem outer corner; join with a sl st in beg ch-1.

Row 3: Rep Row 2. Finish off and weave in ends.

Fringe

Following Fringe instructions on page 9, make single knot fringe. Cut 16″ strands; use 8 strands for each knot. Tie knots evenly spaced (about every 3rd st) across each side of afghan. Trim ends evenly.

Rose Bouquet Bedspread

Size: 77″ × 110″

Materials: Bedspread weight crochet thread, 40, 225-yd
  balls brown; 30, 225-yd balls of various multicolored thread
Size 7 steel crochet hook, or size required for gauge

Gauge: 9 dc = 1″; 5 rows = 1″
      Motif = 5½″

INSTRUCTIONS

First Motif:

With multicolored thread, ch 7, join to form a ring.

Rnd 1: Ch 3 (counts as first dc), work 15 dc in ring; join in 3rd
ch of beg ch-3: 16 dc.

Rnd 2: Ch 5 (counts as first dc and ch-2 sp); * dc in next dc,
ch 2; rep from * 13 times more; join in 3rd ch of beg ch-5:
16 ch-2 sps.

Rnd 3: Sl st in next ch-2 sp, ch 3 (counts as first dc), 2 dc in
same ch-2 sp; * sk next dc, in next ch-2 sp, work 3 dc; rep
from * 14 times more; join in 3rd ch of beg ch-3: 48 dc.

Rnd 4: Ch 5 (counts as first sc and ch 4); * sk next dc, sc in
next dc, ch 4; rep from * 22 times more; join in first ch of beg
ch-5: 24 ch-4 sps.

Rnd 5: Sl st in next ch-4 sp, ch 1, sc in same ch-4 sp; * ch 6,
YO twice, insert hook in next ch-4 sp, YO and draw through:
4 lps on hook; YO and draw through 2 lps on hook: 3 lps rem
on hook; YO and insert hook in next ch-4 sp, YO and draw
through: 5 lps on hook; (YO and draw through 2 lps on hook) 4
times: joined dtrc made; ch 6, sc in next ch-4 sp; rep from
* 7 times more, omit last sc and join in first sc: 8 joined dtrc
sts and 16 ch-6 sps.

Rnd 6: * In next ch-6 sp, work (sc, hdc, dc, 3 trc), dtrc in
next joined dtrc; (YO 3 times, insert hook in next joined dtrc,
YO and draw through: 5 lps on hook; YO and draw through 4
times: dtrc made), in next ch-6 sp work (3 trc, dc, hdc, sc):
petal made; sk next sc; rep from * 7 times more; join in first
sc: 8 petals.

Rnd 7: Ch 1; * work reverse sc (see page 9) in each st of
next petal to the right; rep from * 7 times more; join in first
reverse sc; finish off and weave in ends.

With brown, join in back lps (which were worked over ch-6 sp
of Rnd 5) of 4th st (first trc) of Rnd 6 of any petal.

Rnd 8: * Ch 10, sk next 5 sts of same petal, sl st in back lps
(which were worked over ch-6 sp of Rnd 5) of next trc of
same petal; ch 10, sk next 3 sts of same petal, sk next 3 sts of
next petal, sl st in back lps (which were worked over ch-6 sp
of Rnd 5) of next trc; ch 10, sk next 5 sts of same petal, sl st in
back lps of next trc of same petal; ch 17, sl st in 11th ch from
hook: ch-11 lp made; holding ch-11 lp to your left, work 16 sc
in ch-11 lp: corner lp made, ch 6, sk next 3 sts of same petal,
sk next 3 sts of next petal, sl st in back lps of next trc of same
petal; rep from * 3 times more, work last sl st in beg sl st:
4 corner lps, 8 ch-6 sps, and 12 ch-10 lps.

Rnd 9: Sl st in next 5 chs of next ch-10 lp, ch 6 (counts as first
trc and ch 2), trc in next ch of same ch-10 lp: beg large V-st
made; * † (ch 6, trc in 5th ch of next ch-10 lp, ch 2, trc in next
ch of same ch-10 lp: large V-st made) twice; ch 6, sk next ch-6
sp, dc in 6th sc of next corner lp, ch 2, dc in next sc (7th sc) of
same corner lp: small V-st made: ch 5, sk next 2 sc of same
corner lp, dc in next sc (10th sc): corner sp made, ch 2, dc in
next sc (11th sc) of same corner lp: small V-st made, sk next

5 sc of same corner lp; ch 6, sk next ch-6 sp †, trc in 5th ch of next ch-10 lp, ch 2, trc in next ch of same ch-10 lp; rep from * 2 times more; rep from † to † once; join in 4th ch of beg ch-6: 12 large V-sts, 8 small V-sts, 4 ch-5 corner sps, and 16 ch-6 sps.

Rnd 10: Sl st in ch-2 sp of next large V-st; ch 5 (counts as first dc and ch 2), * dc in 2nd ch of next ch-6 sp, ch 2, sk next 2 chs, dc in 5th ch of same ch-6 sp; (ch 2, dc in next trc of large V-st) twice; ch 2, dc in 2nd ch of next ch-6 sp, ch 2, sk next 2 chs, dc in 5th ch of same ch-6 sp; ch 2, dc in ch-2 sp of next large V-st; ch 2, dc in 2nd ch of next ch-6 sp, ch 2, sk next 2 chs, dc in 5th ch of same ch-6 sp; (ch 2, dc in next dc of small V-st) twice; ch 2, in 3rd ch of next ch-5 corner sp, work (dc, ch 5, dc): corner sp made, (ch 2, dc in next dc of small V-st) twice; ch 2, dc in 2nd ch of next ch-6 sp, ch 2, sk next 2 chs, dc in 5th ch of same ch-6 sp; ch 2, dc in ch-2 sp of next large V-st; rep from * 3 times more, omit last dc and ch 2, join in 3rd ch of beg ch-5: 4 ch-5 corner sps and 68 ch-2 sps.

Rnd 11: Sl st in next 2 chs of next ch-2 sp, sl st in next dc, sl st in next ch-2 sp, ch 3 (counts as first dc), 2 dc in next ch-2 sp; (ch 5, sk next ch-2 sp, 3 dc in next ch-2 sp) 5 times, ch 5, 3 dc in next ch-5 corner sp, ch 5, 3 dc in next ch-2 sp; * (ch 5, sk next ch-2 sp, 3 dc in next ch-2 sp) 8 times, ch 5, 3 dc in next ch-5 corner sp, ch 5, 3 dc in next ch-2 sp; rep from * 2 times more; (ch 5, sk next ch-2 sp, 3 dc in next ch-2 sp) twice, ch 5, join in 3rd ch of beg ch-3: 40 ch-5 sps; finish off and weave in ends.

Second Motif:

Work same as First Motif through Rnd 10. Work last rnd and join First Motif to Second Motif as follows):

Rnd 11: Sl st in next 2 chs of next ch-2 sp, sl st in next dc, ch 3, 3 dc in next ch-2 sp; (ch 5, sk next ch-2 sp, 3 dc in next ch-2 sp) 5 times; ch 5, 3 dc in next ch-5 corner sp; ch 2, hold First Motif and Second Motif with wrong sides tog and Second Motif facing you, sl st in next ch-5 sp to left of 3 dc worked in corner sp of Second Motif, ch 2, 3 dc in next ch-2 sp of Second Motif, ch 2, sk next 3 dc of First Motif, sl st in next ch-5 sp of First Motif, ch 2; (sk next ch-2 sp of Second Motif, 3 dc in next ch-2 sp of Second Motif, ch 2, sk next 3 dc of First Motif, sl st in next ch-5 sp of First Motif; ch 2) 8 times; 3 dc in next ch-5 corner sp of Second Motif, ch 5, 3 dc in next ch-2 sp of Second Motif; working only on Second Motif for remainder of this rnd, * (ch 5, sk next ch-2 sp, 3 dc in next ch-2 sp) 8 times, ch 5, 3 dc in next ch-5 corner sp, ch 5, 3 dc in next ch-2 sp; rep from * once more; (ch 5, sk next ch-2 sp, 3 dc in next ch-2 sp) twice, ch 5, join in 3rd ch of beg ch-3: First and Second Motif joined; finish off and weave in ends.

Remaining Motifs:

Work 278 motifs same as Second Motif continuing to join motifs in last rnd, making 14 rows of motifs with 20 motifs in each row.

Petal Rose Afghan and Pillow

Size: Afghan: about 60″ × 72″ (with ruffle)

Pillow: 12″ × 12″ (without ruffle)

Materials: Caron Wintuk yarn: for afghan, 69 oz off white; 58 oz lt rose; 4 oz spruce. For pillow, 8 oz off white; 4 oz lt rose; 1 oz spruce

Size I aluminum crochet hook, or size required for gauge

12″ pillow form or polyester fiberfill for pillow

Gauge: 1 square = 12″ × 12″

AFGHAN INSTRUCTIONS

Rose Square (make 15)

With lt rose, ch 4, join to form a ring.

Rnd 1: Sl st in ring, ch 4 (counts as an sc and ch 3); (sc in ring, ch 3) 7 times; join in first ch of beg ch-4: 8 ch-3 lps.

Rnd 2: * In next ch-3 sp work (sc, hdc, 3 dc, hdc, sc); rep from * 7 times more; join in beg sc.

Rnd 3: Working behind prev rnd, sl st in first sl st of Rnd 1; ch 5, * sl st in next sc of Rnd 1, ch 5; rep from * 7 times more; sl st in beg sl st.

Rnd 4: * In next ch-5 sp work (sc, hdc, 5 dc, hdc, sc); rep from * 7 times more; join in beg sc.

Rnd 5: Working behind prev rnd, sl st in first sl st of Rnd 3; ch 7, * sl st in next sl st in Rnd 3, ch 7; rep from * 7 times more; sl st in beg sl st.

Rnd 6: * In next ch-7 sp work (sc, hdc, 7 dc, hdc, sc); rep from * 7 times more; join in beg sc.

Rnd 7: Working behind prev rnd, sl st in first sl st of Rnd 5; ch 9, * sl st in next sl st in Rnd 5, ch 9; rep from * 7 times more; sl st in beg sl st.

Rnd 8: * In next ch-9 sp work (sc, hdc, 9 dc, hdc, sc); rep from * 7 times more; join in beg sc; finish off.

Rnd 9: Join spruce in any sl st of Rnd 7; ch 3 (counts as a dc), 2 dc in same st, ch 3; * in next sl st of Rnd 7 work (3 dc, ch 3, 3 dc), ch 3, 3 dc in next sl st of Rnd 7, ch 3; rep from * twice more; in next sl st of Rnd 7 work (3 dc, ch 3, 3 dc), ch 3; join in 3rd ch of beg ch-3; finish off.

Rnd 10: Join off white in any ch-3 sp of (3 dc, ch 3, 3 dc) group on prev rnd; ch 3, dc in same sp: beg of first corner made; (dc in next 3 dc, 3 dc in next ch-3 sp) twice; dc in next 3 dc, * in next ch-3 sp work (2 dc, ch 3, 2 dc): corner made; (dc in next 3 dc, 3 dc in next ch-3 sp) twice; dc in next 3 dc; rep from * twice more; 2 dc in next ch-3 sp, ch 3; join in 3rd ch of beg ch-3: first corner completed.

Rnd 11: Ch 3, * dc in each dc across side, in next ch-3 corner sp work (2 dc, ch 3, 2 dc); rep from * 4 times more; join in 3rd ch of beg ch-3.

Rnd 12: Ch 3, * dc in each dc across side, in next ch-3 corner sp work (2 dc, ch 3, 2 dc): corner made; rep from * 3 times more; dc in next 2 dc; join in 3rd ch of beg ch-3.

Rnd 13: Ch 3, * dc in each dc across side, in next ch-3 corner sp work (2 dc, ch 3, 2 dc): corner made; rep from * 3 times more; dc in next 4 dc; join in 3rd ch of beg ch-3.

Rnd 14: Ch 3, * dc in each dc across side, in next ch-3 corner sp work (2 dc, ch 3, 2 dc): corner made; rep from * 3 times more; dc in next 6 dc; join in 3rd ch of beg ch-3.

Rnd 15: Ch 3, * dc in each dc across side, in next ch-3 corner sp work (2 dc, ch 3, 2 dc); rep from * 3 times more; dc in next 8 dc; join in 3rd ch of beg ch-3; finish off.

Solid Block (make 15)

With off white, ch 4, join to form a ring.

Rnd 1: Ch 3 (counts as a dc in this and all following rnds), 2 dc in ring, (ch 3, 3 dc in ring) 3 times; ch 3; join in 3rd ch of beg ch-3.

Rnd 2: Ch 3, * dc in each dc to next ch-3 sp, in next ch-3 sp work (2 dc, ch 3, 2 dc): corner made; rep from * 3 times more; join in 3rd ch of beg ch-3.

Rnd 3: Ch 3, * dc in each dc to next ch-3 sp, in next ch-3 sp work (2 dc, ch 3, 2 dc): corner made; rep from * 3 times more; dc in next 2 dc; join in 3rd ch of beg ch-3: 7 dc between corners.

Rnd 4: Ch 3, * dc in each dc to next ch-3 sp, in next ch-3 sp work (2 dc, ch 3, 2 dc): corner made; rep from * 3 times more; dc in next 4 dc; join in 3rd ch of beg ch-3: 11 dc between corners.

Rnd 5: Ch 3, * dc in each dc to next ch-3 sp, in next ch-3 sp work (2 dc, ch 3, 2 dc): corner made; rep from * 3 times more; dc in next 6 dc; join in 3rd ch of beg ch-3: 15 dc between corners.

Rnd 6: Ch 3, * dc in each dc to next ch-3 sp, in next ch-3 sp work (2 dc, ch 3, 2 dc): corner made; rep from * 3 times more; dc in next 8 dc; join in 3rd ch of beg ch-3: 19 dc between corners.

Rnd 7: Ch 3, * dc in each dc to next ch-3 sp, in next ch-3 sp work (2 dc, ch 3, 2 dc): corner made; rep from * 3 times more; dc in next 10 dc; join in 3rd ch of beg ch-3: 23 dc between corners.

Rnd 8: Ch 3, * dc in each dc to next ch-3 sp work (2 dc, ch 3, 2 dc): corner made; rep from * 3 times more; dc in next 12 dc; join in 3rd ch of beg ch-3: 27 dc between corners.

Rnd 9: Ch 3, * dc in each dc to next ch-3 sp work (2 dc, ch 3, 2 dc): corner made; rep from * 3 times more; dc in next 14 dc; join in 3rd ch of beg ch-3: 31 dc between corners.

Rnd 10: Ch 3, * dc in each dc to next ch-3 sp work (2 dc, ch 3, 2 dc): corner made; rep from * 3 times more; dc in next 16 dc; join in 3rd ch of beg ch-3: 35 dc between corners; finish off.

Assembling

Join squares in 6 rows of 5 squares, referring to Diagram A for placement of squares. To join squares, hold 2 squares with right sides tog. Carefully matching sts on both squares and with off white, sew with overcast st in inner lps (see page 10) only across side, beg and ending with one corner st and being sure that all four-corner junctions are firmly joined.

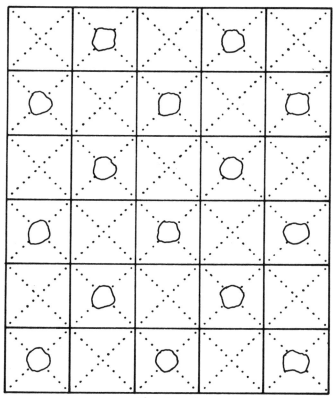

Diagram A

Ruffle

Hold afghan with right side facing you; join off white in ch-3 corner sp of any corner.

Rnd 1: Ch 3 (counts as a dc in this and all following rnds), in same sp work (2 dc, ch 3, 3 dc), * sk next 2 dc, in next dc work (3 dc, ch 3, 3 dc); rep from * around afghan, adjusting sts slightly so that a (3 dc, ch 3, 3 dc) is worked in ch-3 corner sp of each rem outer corner; join in 3rd ch of beg ch-3.

Rnd 2: Ch 3, sk next 2 dc, in next ch-3 sp work (3 dc, ch 3, 3 dc); * sk next 2 dc, dc in next dc, sk next 3 dc, in next ch-3 sp work (3 dc, ch 3, 3 dc); rep from * around; join in 3rd ch of beg ch-3.

Rnd 3: Ch 3, in next ch-3 sp work (3 dc, ch 3, 3 dc); * dc in next dc, in next ch-3 sp work (3 dc, ch 3, 3 dc); rep from * around; join in 3rd ch of beg ch-3.

Rnd 4: Rep Rnd 3. Finish off.

Rnd 5: Join lt rose in any dc; ch 1, sc in same dc as joining, sc in each st around afghan; join in beg sc; finish off and weave in ends.

PILLOW INSTRUCTIONS

Following instructions for squares in afghan instructions, make 1 rose square and 1 solid square.

Assembling

Hold squares with wrong sides tog, carefully matching sts. Join off white in first dc in upper right-hand corner; work sc thru same dc as joining and at the same time thru same dc on back square; working thru matching sts on both squares, sc in each dc and 3 dc in each ch-3 outer corner sp around 3 sides of pillow; insert pillow form; continue across 4th side; join in beg sc.

Ruffle

Rnd 1: Ch 3 (counts as a dc in this and all following rnds), in same sp work (2 dc, ch 3, 3 dc), * sk next 2 sc, in next sc work (3 dc, ch 3, 3 dc); rep from * around afghan, adjusting sts slightly so that a (3 dc, ch 3, 3 dc) is worked in ch-3 corner sp of each rem outer corner; join in 3rd ch of beg ch-3.

Rnd 2: Ch 3, sk next 2 dc, in next ch-3 sp work (3 dc, ch 3, 3 dc); * sk next 2 dc, dc in next dc, sk next 3 dc, in next ch-3 sp work (3 dc, ch 3, 3 dc); rep from * around; join in 3rd ch of beg ch-3.

Rnd 3: Ch 3, in next ch-3 sp work (3 dc, ch 3, 3 dc); * dc in next dc, in next ch-3 sp work (3 dc, ch 3, 3 dc); rep from * around; join in 3rd ch of beg ch-3; finish off.

Rnd 4: Join lt rose in any dc; ch 1, sc in same dc as joining, sc in each st around afghan; join in beg sc; finish off and weave in ends.

Diagonal Diamonds Granny

DESIGNED BY RITA WEISS

Size: About 48″ × 64″ before fringing

This afghan sports a new look for a granny—a diagonal stripe arrangement that forms inset diamonds. The technique is a little different than most granny squares, and is fun to do.

Materials: Worsted weight yarn, 23 oz dusty rose; 23 oz cream; 9 oz dk blue

Size J aluminum crochet hook, or size required for gauge

Gauge: One square = 4″

Special Note: When changing colors, work until 2 lps of last color remain on hook; with new color, YO and draw through 2 lps on hook.

INSTRUCTIONS

Square (make 192)

With blue, ch 4.

Rnd 1 (right side): 11 dc in 4th ch from hook; join with a sl st in 3rd ch of beg ch-4: 12 dc (counting first 3 chs as dc in this and all following rnds); finish off blue.

Rnd 2 (wrong side): Holding Rnd 1 with wrong side facing you, join rose with a sl st in any dc; ch 3, dc in same dc; dc in next 2 dc, 4 dc in next dc, dc in next 2 dc, 2 dc in next dc, changing to cream on last dc; drop rose in front of work; with cream, 2 dc in same dc as last 2 rose dc; dc in next 2 dc, 4 dc in next dc, dc in next 2 dc, 2 dc in same dc as beg 2 rose dc; join with sl st in 3rd ch of beg ch-3; ch 3 (counts as first dc of next rnd, *turn work.*

Rnd 3 (right side): 2 dc in joining sl st of prev rnd; † dc in next 5 dc, in next dc work (3 dc, ch 1, 3 dc); dc in next 5 dc †; 3 dc in next dc, changing to rose on last dc (use yarn dropped on wrong side of last rnd); finish off cream; ch 1, 3 dc in same dc as last 3 cream dc; rep from † to † once; 3 dc in same dc as first 2 cream dc of rnd, ch 1; join with a sl st in 3rd ch of beg ch-3; finish off and weave in ends.

Assembling

Join squares as shown in Diagram A. To join squares, hold two squares with right sides tog. Carefully matching sts on both squares and with matching yarn, sew with overcast st in bls only (see page 10) across side, beg and ending with one

corner st and being sure all four-corner junctions are firmly joined.

Diagram A

Fringe

Following Fringe instructions on page 9, make spaghetti knot fringe. Cut 16″ strands. Matching yarn with edge st, tie a knot in each st across each short end of afghan. Trim ends evenly.

Country Granny

DESIGNED BY JEAN LEINHAUSER

Size: About 50″ × 70″ before fringing

This is a traditional granny square, dressed up in fresh new country colors rather than the old black-with-brights combination. It's just as cozy and comfortable, but a prettier decorative accent.

Materials: Worsted weight yarn, 43 oz tan; 21 oz country blue; 10 oz dusty rose; 3 oz dk rose
Size I aluminum crochet hook, or size required for gauge

Gauge: 4 dc = 1″
One 9-rnd square = 10″

INSTRUCTIONS

Granny square (make 35)

With dk rose, ch 4, join with a sl st to form a ring.

Rnd 1: Ch 3 (counts as dc in this and all following rnds), 2 dc in ring; (ch 2 3 dc in ring) 3 times; ch 2; join with a sl st in 3rd ch of beg ch-3; finish off dk rose.

Rnd 2: Join blue with a sl st in any ch-2 sp; ch 3, in same sp work (2 dc, ch 2, 3 dc): corner made; * in next ch-2 sp work (3 dc, ch 2, 3 dc): corner made; rep from * twice more; join with a sl st in 3rd ch of beg ch-3; finish off blue.

Rnd 3: Join dusty rose with a sl st in any ch-2 corner sp; ch 3, in same sp work (2 dc, ch 2, 3 dc): corner made; * 3 dc between next two 3-dc groups for side, in next ch-2 corner sp work (3 dc, ch 2, 3 dc): corner made; rep from * twice more; 3 dc between next two 3-dc groups for last side; join with a sl st in 3rd ch of beg ch-3. Do not finish off.

Rnd 4: Sl st in next 2 dc and into ch-2 corner sp; ch 3, in same sp work (2 dc, ch 2, 3 dc): corner made; * 3 dc between each pair of 3-dc groups along side, in next ch-2 corner sp work (3 dc, ch 2, 3 dc): corner made; rep from * twice more; 3 dc between each pair of 3-dc groups along last side; join with a sl st in 3rd ch of beg ch-3; finish off dusty rose.

Rnd 5: Join tan with a sl st in any ch-2 corner sp; ch 3, in same sp work (2 dc, ch 2, 3 dc): corner made; * 3 dc between each pair of 3-dc groups along side, in next ch-2 corner sp work (3 dc, ch 2, 3 dc): corner made; rep from * twice more;

3 dc between each pair of 3-dc groups along last side; join with a sl st in 3rd ch of beg ch-3; finish off tan.

Rnd 6: With blue, rep Rnd 5, but at end of rnd, do not finish off blue.

Rnd 7: With blue, rep Rnd 4.

Rnd 8: With tan, rep Rnd 5, but at end of rnd, do not finish off tan.

Rnd 9: With tan, rep Rnd 4. Weave in ends.

Assembling

Join squares in 7 rows of 5 squares. To join squares, hold two squares with right sides tog. Carefully matching sts on both squares and with tan, sew with overcast st in bls only (see page 10) across side, beg and ending with one corner st. Join squares in rows; then sew rows tog in same manner, being sure that all four-corner junctions are firmly joined.

Finishing

Edging: With right side of afghan facing you, join tan with a sl st in ch-2 sp of upper right-hand corner.

Rnd 1: Ch 3 (counts as a dc in this and following rnd), in same sp as joining work (2 dc, ch 2, 3 dc): corner made; along each side of afghan, work 3 dc between each pair of 3-dc groups and in corner sp on each side of row joinings; in each rem outer ch-2 corner sp of afghan, work (3 dc, ch 2, 3 dc): corner made; join with a sl st in 3rd ch of beg ch-3.

Rnd 2: Sl st in next 2 dc and into corner sp; ch 3, in same corner sp work (2 dc, ch 2, 3 dc); along each side, work 3 dc between each pair of 3-dc groups; in each rem corner sp work (3 dc, ch 2, 3 dc); join with a sl st in 3rd ch of beg ch-3; finish off.

Fringe

Following Fringe instructions on page 9, make triple knot fringe. Cut 30″ strands of tan; use 6 strands for each knot of fringe. Tie knots between each 3-dc group across each short end of afghan. Then work double and triple knots per instructions. Trim ends evenly.

Rnd 4: TURN; sk last cluster of prev rnd, join white with a sl st in next sc; ch 1, sc in same sc as joining, * hdc in next st, dc in next st, dc in next st, in next st work (dc, ch 1, trc, ch 1, dc): corner made; dc in next st; hdc in next st, sc in next 4 sts; rep from * around, ending last rep by working sc in last 3 sts; join with a sl st in beg sc. Do not finish off.

Rnd 5: Ch 3, do NOT turn; dc in next 3 sts; * ch 2, sk ch-1 sp, in next trc work (dc, ch 1, trc, ch 1, dc): corner made; ch 2, sk ch-1 sp, dc in next 10 sts; rep from * around, ending last rep by working dc in last 6 sts; join with a sl st in 3rd ch of beg ch-3.

Rnd 6: Ch 3, do NOT turn; dc in next 3 dc; * ch 2, sk ch-2 sp, in next trc work (dc, ch 2, trc, ch 2, dc): corner made; ch 2, sk ch-2 sp, dc in next 10 dc; rep from * around, ending last rep by working dc in last 6 dc; join in 3rd ch of beg ch-3; finish off and weave in ends.

Assembling

Join squares in 8 rows of 6 squares. To join squares, hold two squares with right sides tog. Carefully matching sts on both squares and with white, sew with overcast st in bls only (see page 10) across side, beg and ending with one corner st. Join squares in rows; then sew rows tog in same manner, being sure that all four-corner junctions are firmly joined.

Edging

Rnd 1: Holding afghan with right side facing you, join white with a sl st in corner trc of upper right-hand corner; 3 sc in same trc, 2 sc in ch-2 sp, sc in dc, 3 sc in ch-2 sp, sc in next 10 dc; 3 sc in ch-2 sp; sc in next dc, 2 sc in ch-2 sp, sc in joining; continue in this manner around afghan, working 3 sc in trc of each outer corner; join with a sl st in beg sc.

Rnd 2: Sc in each sc around, working 3 sc in center st of each outer corner; finish off and weave in ends.

Fringe

Following Fringe instructions on page 9, make double knot fringe. Cut 20″ strands; use 6 strands for each knot. Tie knots evenly spaced (about every 3rd st) across each short end of afghan. Then work double knots per instructions. Trim ends evenly.

Delft Tiles
DESIGNED BY JEAN LEINHAUSER

Size: About 45″ × 60″ before fringing

It's hard to improve on the fresh, good looks of blue and white Delft tiles. Jean says this afghan was inspired by memories of drinking hot Dutch chocolate in a warm Dutch kitchen.

Materials: Worsted weight yarn, 9 oz dk blue; 10 oz lt blue; 32 oz white

Size I aluminum crochet hook, or size required for gauge

Gauge: 3 dc = 1″
One square = 7½″

Stitch Note: CLUSTER. (YO, insert hook in st, hook yarn and draw through st; YO and draw through 2 lps on hook) 3 times: 4 lps on hook; YO and draw through all lps on hook, pushing cluster to right side of work: cluster made.

INSTRUCTIONS

Square (make 48)

With dk blue, ch 4, join with a sl st to form a ring.

Rnd 1 (wrong side): Ch 3 (counts as a dc), 11 dc in ring; join with a sl st in 3rd ch of beg ch-3: 12 dc. Finish off dk blue.

Rnd 2 (right side): TURN; join lt blue with a sl st in any dc; ch 4 (counts as a trc), trc in same dc as joining, trc in sp between last dc and next dc; * 2 trc in next dc, trc in sp between last dc and next dc; rep from * around; join with a sl st in 4th ch of beg ch-4; 36 trc. Finish off lt blue.

Rnd 3: TURN; join dk blue with a sl st in last trc of prev rnd; ch 1, sc in same trc as joining, sc in next trc, in next trc work cluster; * sc in next 2 trc, work cluster in next trc; rep from * around; join with a sl st in beg sc: 12 clusters. Finish off dk blue.

Chapter 3
GRANNY'S KIDS

What fun to crochet colorful grannys for the youngest members of the family!

This chapter includes a complete layette, a gorgeous afghan, and several styles for older children.

Blue Jumper and Shawl

Sizes:

Child Size	4	6	8	10
Finished jumper width around underarms:	22″	24″	26″	28″
Finished Jumper length from shoulder to knee:	24″	26″	28″	30″

Materials: Baby weight yarn, Dark Blue (not including Granny Squares):

Child Size	4	6	8	10
	10 oz	12 oz	13 oz	16 oz

For Granny Squares only for all sizes: 1 oz each of Dark Blue, Pink and Dark Pink.

Size O steel crochet hook, or size required for gauge.

Gauge: 13 hdc = 2″; 10 rows = 2″
3-rnd square = 2″

INSTRUCTIONS

Note: Instructions are written for Size 4 with changes for Size 6, 8, and 10 in parentheses.

Make 17 (19, 20, 21) squares in dark blue, 17 (18, 20, 21) squares in pink, and 17 (17, 19, 19) in dark pink for a total of 51 (54, 59, 61) squares (3-rnd Traditional Granny Square #2 on page 12) for jumper and shawl.

Joining Squares

Refer to Color Key and Diagrams 1 through 4 for arranging squares for jumper and shawl. Hold 2 squares with wrong sides together. Carefully matching sts, with dark blue, sew with overcast st in inner lps only (page 10) in each st across, ending in opposite corner of square. Continue to join squares together referring to Diagrams 1 through 4 for color arrangement. Sew first and last square of strip together of Top Jumper Squares and Bottom Jumper Squares to form a circle.

Jumper Front

With dark blue, ch 126 (139, 150, 163).

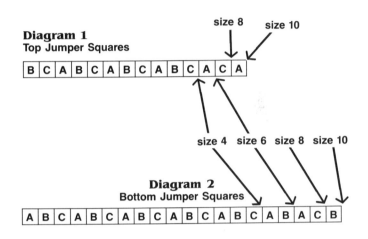

Diagram 1
Top Jumper Squares

size 8   size 10

B C A B C A B C A B C A C A

size 4   size 6   size 8   size 10

Diagram 2
Bottom Jumper Squares

A B C A B C A B C A B C A B A C B

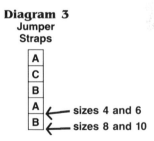

Diagram 3
Jumper Straps

A
C
B
A ← sizes 4 and 6
B ← sizes 8 and 10

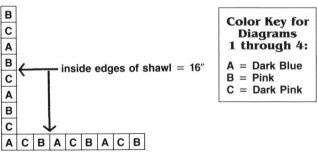

Diagram 4
Shawl

B
C
A
B ← inside edges of shawl = 16″
C
A
B
C
A C B A C B A C B

Color Key for Diagrams 1 through 4:
A = Dark Blue
B = Pink
C = Dark Pink

Row 1: Hdc in 2nd ch from hook, hdc in each ch: 125 (138, 149, 162) hdc; ch 2 (counts as first hdc in next and following rows), turn.

Row 2: Sk first hdc; * hdc between next 2 hdc, sk next hdc; rep from * to last hdc, hdc in turning ch-2: 125 (138, 149, 162) hdc; ch 2, turn.

Row 3: Sk first hdc, YO and insert hook in sp under lps and between next hdc, YO and draw through (3 lps on hook), sk next hdc, YO and insert hook in sp under lps and between next hdc, YO and draw through: 5 lps on hook, YO and draw through all lps on hook: beg hdc-dec made; * sk next hdc, hdc in sp under lps and between next hdc; rep from * to last hdc and turning ch-2; sk next hdc, YO and insert hook in sp under lps and between next hdc, YO and draw through (3 lps on hook), YO and insert hook in sp under lps and between next hdc and turning ch-2, YO and draw through (5 lps on hook), YO and draw through all lps on hook: end hdc-dec made: 123 (136, 147, 160) hdc; ch 2, turn.

Rows 4 through 6: Rep Row 2: 121 (134, 145, 158) hdc; ch 2, turn.

Rep Rows 4 through 6 until you have 77 (84, 91, 98) hdc; place marker at end of this row.

Rep Row 2 until piece measures 4″ (4½″, 4½″, 5″) from marker at end of Row 72 (81, 87, 96); finish off and weave in ends.

Jumper Back

Work same as Jumper Front.

Jumper Assembly

Hold jumper front and back with right sides together and pin at both side edges in several places. Carefully matching sts, with dark blue, sew with overcast st in inner lps only (page 10) in each st across.

Place jumper on flat surface and pin at bottom and stop side seams. Fold jumper, matching pins in center, and pin again at top and bottom side edges, dividing top and bottom edge into fourths. Rep in same manner for Top and Bottom Jumper granny square pieces (previously assembled). With right sides together, matching pins, pin granny squares to top and bottom of jumper. With dark blue, sew granny squares to jumper with overcast st.

With dark blue, sew straps into desired place on jumper with wrong sides together, using overcast st.

Neck Edging: With right side facing, join dark blue at left hand corner of neck edge in seam joining granny squares. Edging will begin at strap of jumper.

Rnd 1: Ch 1; * sc in ch-2 corner of sp of next granny square; † sc in next 3 dc, sc in next ch-1 sp †; rep from † to † once; sc in next 3 dc, sc in next ch-2 corner sp, sc in seam; rep from * 3 (3, 4, 4) times more; continue to work in same manner across top jumper edge, strap and opposite top jumper edge; join in first sc; ch 1.

Rnd 2: Sc in each sc; join in first sc; finish off and weave in ends.

Armhole Edging: With right side facing, join dark blue at left hand corner of armhole edge in seam joining granny squares. Edging will begin at strap of jumper.

Rnd 1: Work same as Rnd 1 of Neck Edging, working across strap and top jumper edge; join in first sc; ch 1.

Rnd 2: Rep Rnd 2 of Neck Edging.

Bottom Edging: Hold jumper with bottom edge on top and with right side facing; join dark blue at bottom edge in seam joining granny squares.

Rnd 1: Ch 1; * sc in ch-2 corner sp of next granny square; † sc in next 3 dc, sc in next ch-1 sp †; rep from † to † once; sc in next 3 dc, sc in next ch-2 corner sp, sc in seam; rep from * 14 (16, 18, 19) times more; join in first sc; ch 1.

Rnd 2: Sc in each sc; join in first sc; finish off and weave in ends.

Shawl

Shawl Body: With dark blue, ch 3.

Row 1: 3 hdc in 3rd ch from hook: 4 hdc; ch 2 (counts as first hdc in next and following rows), turn.

Row 2: Sk first hdc, 2 hdc in sp under lps and between first and 2nd hdc; sk next hdc, hdc in sp under lps and between next 2 hdc; 2 hdc in sp under lps and between next hdc and turning ch-2: 6 hdc; ch 2, turn.

Row 3: Sk first hdc, 2 hdc between first and 2nd hdc; (sk next hdc, hdc in sp under lps and between next 2 hdc) 3 times; 2 hdc in sp under lps and between next hdc and turning ch-2: 8 hdc; ch 2, turn.

Row 4: Sk first hdc, 2 hdc in sp under lps and between first and 2nd hdc; (sk next hdc, hdc in sp under lps and between next 2 hdc) 5 times; 2 hdc in sp under lps and between next hdc and turning ch-2: 10 hdc; ch 2, turn.

Row 5: Sk first hdc, 2 hdc in sp under lps and between first and 2nd hdc; † sk next hdc, hdc in sp under lps and between next 2 hdc †; rep from † to † to last hdc and turning ch-2; 2 hdc in sp between last hdc and turning ch-2: 12 hdc; ch 2, turn.

Rep Row 5 (working 2 incs for each row) until side edges of shawl body measures 16″, or same as inside edges of assembled granny squares; finish off and weave in ends.

Shawl Assembly

With wrong sides tog and matching inside edges of assembled granny squares and side edges of shawl body, with dark blue, sew with overcast st in inner lps only (page 10), keeping work flat.

Shawl Edging: Hold shawl with right side facing and widest edge on top and join dark blue in ch-2 corner sp of granny square on right-hand side; ch 1.

Rnd 1: 3 sc in ch-2 corner sp; (sc in next 3 dc, sc in next ch-1 sp) twice, sc in next 3 dc; sc in next ch-2 corner sp, sc in seam; sc in each hdc of shawl body; sc in seam, sc in next ch-2 corner sp, (sc in next 3 dc, sc in next ch-1 sp) twice, sc in next 3 dc, 3 sc in next ch-2 corner sp; * † (sc in next 3 dc, sc in next ch-1 sp) 2 times, sc in next 3 dc, sc in next ch-2 corner sp, sc in seam, sc in next ch-2 corner sp †; rep from * 8 times more; in same ch-2 corner sp, work 2 sc (3 sc in ch-2 corner sp); rep from † to † 8 times; (sc in next 3 dc, sc in next ch-1 sp) twice, sc in next 3 dc; join in first sc; ch 1.

Rnd 2: Sc in each sc; join in first sc; finish off and weave in ends.

Pretty Punkin Baby Afghan, Cardigan and Bonnet

AFGHAN

Size: About 26½″ × 23″

Materials: Sport weight yarn, 3 oz dk orange; 3 oz orange; 2 oz white; 1 oz brown
Size D aluminum crochet hook, or size required for gauge

Gauge: 6-rnd square = 3½″ × 3½″

AFGHAN INSTRUCTIONS

Square (make 42)

With orange, ch 4, join to form a ring.

Rnd 1: Ch 1, 12 sc in ring; join in beg sc; finish off.

Rnd 2: Join brown in any sc; ch 1, sc in same sc as joining, sc in each sc; join in beg sc: 12 sc. Do not turn; work in rnds.

Rnd 3: Ch 1, sc in each sc; join in beg sc; finish off.

Rnd 4: Join white in any sc; ch 3 (counts as a dc in this and all following rnds), holding back last lp of each dc on hook, work 2 dc in same sc, YO and draw through all 3 lps on hook: cluster made; * ch 3, holding back last lp of each dc on hook, work 3 dc in next sc, YO and draw through all 4 lps on hook: cluster made; rep from * 10 times more; ch 3; join in 3rd ch of beg ch-3: 12 clusters; finish off.

Rnd 5: Join orange in any ch-3 sp; ch 3, in same sp work (2 dc, ch 3, 3 dc): corner made; * (sk next cluster, 3 dc in next ch-3 sp) twice; sk next cluster, in next ch-3 sp work (3 dc, ch 3, 3 dc): corner made; rep from * twice more; (sk next cluster, 3 dc in next ch-3 sp) twice; join in 3rd ch of beg ch-3: 12 dc between ch-3 corner sps; finish off.

Rnd 6: Join dk orange in any ch-3 corner sp; ch 3, in same sp work (2 dc, ch 3, 3 dc): corner made; * (3 dc between next pair of dc-groups) 3 times; in next ch-3 corner sp work (3 dc, ch 3, 3 dc): corner made; rep from * twice more; (3 dc between next pair of dc-groups) 3 times; join in 3rd ch of beg ch-3: 15 dc between ch-3 corner sps; finish off and weave in ends.

Assembling

Join squares in 7 rows of 6 squares. To join squares, hold two squares with right sides tog. Carefully matching sts on both squares and with dk orange, sew with overcast st in inner lps (see page 10) only across side, beg and ending with one corner st. Join squares in rows; then sew rows tog in same manner, being sure all four-corner junctions are firmly joined.

Edging

Hold afghan with right side facing you; join white in ch-3 corner sp of upper right-hand corner.

Rnd 1: Ch 1, 3 sc in same sp; sc in each dc and each joining around afghan, working 3 sc in each ch-3 sp of each rem outer corner sp; join in beg sc; finish off.

Rnd 2: Join orange in center sc of any 3-sc outer corner group; ch 1, 3 sc in same sp, sc in each sc around, working 3 sc in center sc of each rem outer corner; join in beg sc; finish off.

Rnd 3: With brown, rep Rnd 2.

Rnd 4: With dk orange, rep Rnd 2. Weave in all ends.

CARDIGAN AND BONNET

Size: 3 (6–9) months

Materials: Sport weight yarn, 7 oz orange; 1 oz white; 1 oz brown
Size D aluminum crochet hook, or size required for gauge
Three ⅝″ diameter white buttons

Gauge: 4-rnd square = 2½″
20 hdc = 4″
15 hdc rows = 4″

CARDIGAN INSTRUCTIONS

Square (make 15 [16–17])

With orange, ch 4, join with a sl st to form a ring.

Rnd 1: Ch 1, 12 sc in ring; join in beg sc; finish off.

Rnd 2: Join brown in any sc; ch 1, sc in same sc as joining; sc in each sc; join in beg sc: 12 sc; finish off.

Rnd 3: Join white in any sc; ch 3 (counts as a dc in this and all following rnds), holding back last lp of each dc on hook, work 2 dc in same sc, YO and draw through all 3 lps on hook: cluster made; * ch 3, holding back last lp of each dc on hook, work 3 dc in next sc, YO and draw through all 4 lps on hook: cluster made; rep from * 10 times more; ch 3; join with a sl st in 3rd ch of beg ch-3: 12 clusters; finish off.

Rnd 4: Join orange in any ch-3 sp; ch 1, in same sp work (3 sc, ch 3, 3 sc): corner made; * (sk next cluster, 3 sc in next ch-3 sp) twice; sk next cluster, in next ch-3 sp work (3 sc, ch 3, 3 sc): corner made; rep from * twice more; (sk next cluster, 3 sc in next ch-3 sp) twice; join in beg sc: 12 sc between ch-4 corner sps; finish off.

Joining

Join 9 (10–11) squares tog for bottom border of cardigan and join 3 squares tog for each sleeve border. To join squares, hold two squares with right sides tog. Carefully matching sts on both squares and with orange, sew with overcast st in inner lps (see page 10) only across side, beg and ending with one corner st.

Cardigan Body

Hold bottom border with right side facing you and long edge at top; join orange in ch-3 corner sp of upper right-hand corner.

Row 1 (right side): Ch 2 (counts as a hdc), * † hdc in next 3 sc; (sk next sc, hdc in next 2 sc) 3 times; hdc in next ch-3 corner sp †; hdc in joining, hdc in ch-3 corner sp of next square; rep from * 7 (8–9) times more, then rep from † to † once: 107 (119–131) hdc; ch 2, turn.

Row 2: Sk first hdc, hdc in each hdc; ch 2, turn.

Rep Row 2 until cardigan measures 5″ (6″–7″) from beg of border. Set aside.

Sleeves (make 2)

Hold sleeve border with right side facing you and long edge at top; join orange in ch-3 corner sp of upper right-hand corner.

Row 1 (right side): Ch 2 (counts as a hdc); * † hdc in next 3 sc; (sk next sc, hdc in next 2 sc) 3 times; hdc in next ch-3 sp †; hdc in joining, hdc in ch-3 corner sp of next square; rep from * once more, then rep from † to † once: 35 hdc; ch 2 (counts as a dc in next row), turn.

Row 2: Sk first hdc, hdc in each hdc; ch 2 (counts as a hdc in next row), turn.

Row 3: Rep Row 2.

Row 4: Sk first hdc, 2 hdc in next hdc: inc made; hdc in each hdc across to last hdc, 2 hdc in last hdc: inc made: 37 hdc; ch 2 (counts as a hdc in next row), turn.

Rows 5 through 7: Rep Row 2.

Row 8: Rep Row 4.

Rep Rows 5 through 8 in sequence once (3 times–5 times). At end of Row 12 (20–28): 41 (45–49) hdc.

Work even until sleeve measures 5½″ (6″–6½″) including border. Finish off.

Yoke

Hold cardigan with right side facing you and border at the bottom; join orange in first hdc at top right-hand edge.

Row 1: Ch 1, sc in next 26 (29–31) hdc; holding sleeve with right side facing you and border at bottom, sk first 2 hdc on sleeve, sc in next 37 (41–45) hdc on sleeve, sk last 2 hdc on sleeve; sk next 4 hdc on cardigan, sc in next 47 (53–61) hdc on cardigan; holding rem sleeve with right side facing you, sk first 2 hdc on sleeve, sc in next 37 (41–45) hdc on sleeve, sk last 2 hdc on sleeve; sk next 4 hdc on cardigan, sc in next 26 (29–31) hdc: 173 (193–213); ch 1, turn.

Row 2: Sc in each sc; ch 1, turn.

Note: Raglan seam decreases beg in following row.

Row 3: Sc in next 25 (28–30) sc; sk next 2 sc, sc in next 35 (39–43) sc; sk next 2 sc, sc in next 45 (51–59) sc; sk next 2 sc, sc in next 35 (39–43) sc; sk next 2 sc, sc in next 25 (28–30) sc: 165 (185–205) sc; ch 1, turn.

Row 4: Rep Row 2.

Row 5: Sc in next 24 (27–29) sc; sk next 2 sc, sc in next 33 (37–41) sc; sk next 2 sc, sc in next 43 (49–57) sc; sk next 2 sc, sc in next 33 (37–41) sc; sk next 2 sc, sc in next 24 (27–29) sc: 157 (177–197) sc; ch 1, turn.

Row 6: Rep Row 2.

Rep Rows 5 and 6, 8 (9–10) times, keeping raglan decreases over prev ones.

Neck Shaping

Row 1: Sl st in next 3 sc, sc in next 12 (14–15) sc; sk next 2 sc, sc in next 15 (17–19) sc; sk next 2 sc, sc in next 25 (29–35) sc; sk next 2 sc, sc in next 15 (19–22) sc; sk next 2 sc, sc in next 12 (14–15) sc; ch 1, turn.

Row 2: Sl st in next 2 sc, sc in next 75 (87–99) sc; ch 1, turn.

Row 3: Sc in next 9 (10–12) sc; sk next 2 sc, sc in next 13 (15–17) sc; sk next 2 sc, sc in next 23 (27–33) sc; sk next 2 sc, sc in next 13 (15–17) sc; sk next 2 sc, sc in next 9 (11–12) sc: 67 (79–91) sc; ch 1, turn.

Row 4: Sc in each sc; finish off.

Assembling

Sew sleeve seams and short underarm seams as follows. With orange and yarn needle and with wrong sides tog, carefully match sts and sew seams with backstitching through both lps of corresponding sts.

Edging

Hold cardigan with right side facing you and border at top; join orange with a sl st in center sc of right-hand corner.

Rnd 1: Ch 1, sc in same sc as joining, sc in each sc and joining across to next 3-sc outer corner; sc in next sc, 3 sc in next sc, sc in each sc across border; continuing around cardigan body to opposite border, sc in each row of right front edge, 3 sc in next corner st, sc around neck edge, 3 sc in next corner st, sc in each row of left front edge, sc in each sc of border; join in beg sc.

Rnd 2: Ch 1, sc in same sc as joining, sc in each sc around cardigan, working three buttonholes in right front edge, the first about 3½″ from lower edge and upper one about ½″ from beg of neck edging (to work buttonhole: ch 2, sk next 2 sc: buttonhole made); join in beg sc; finish off.

Rnd 3: Join brown in same sc as joining of prev rnd; ch 1, sc in same st, sc in each sc and ch around cardigan; join in beg sc; finish off and weave in ends.

Sew buttons on left front edge to correspond with buttonholes.

Sleeve Borders

With right side of sleeve facing you, join orange in seam.

Rnd 1: Ch 1, sc in each sc and joining around border; join in beg sc.

Rnd 2: Ch 1, sc in same sc as joining, sc in each sc; join in beg sc; finish off.

Rnd 3: Join brown in same st as joining of prev rnd; sc in each sc; join in beg sc; finish off and weave in ends.

Rep for other sleeve.

BONNET INSTRUCTIONS

Square (make 5)

Refer to square directions for cardigan.

Border

Join squares in same manner as border of cardigan. Set aside.

Crown

With orange, ch 4, join with a sl st to form a ring.

Rnd 1: Ch 2 (counts as a hdc in this and all following rnds), 15 hdc in ring; join in 2nd ch of beg ch-2: 16 hdc.

Rnd 2: Ch 2, (2 hdc in next hdc, hdc in next hdc) 7 times; 2 hdc in next hdc; join in 2nd ch of beg ch-2: 24 hdc.

Note: Following rnds are not joined. Turn at end of each rnd.

Rnd 3: Ch 2, hdc in same st as joining, 2 hdc in each hdc; join with a sl st in 2nd ch of beg ch-2: 48 hdc; ch 2 (counts as a hdc in next rnd), turn.

Rnd 4: Hdc in next hdc, (2 hdc in next hdc, hdc in next 2 hdc) 15 times; 2 hdc in next hdc; join in 2nd ch of turning ch-2: 64 hdc; ch 2 (counts as a hdc in next rnd), turn.

Rnd 5: Hdc in next 2 hdc, (2 hdc in next hdc, hdc in next 3 hdc) 15 times; 2 hdc in next hdc; join in 2nd ch of beg ch-2: 80 hdc; ch 2 (counts as a hdc in next rnd), turn.

Rep Rnd 5, 5 (6–6) times, having 1 more hdc between each inc. At end of Rnd 10 (11–11): 160 (176–176) hdc.

Rnd 11 (12–12): Hdc in each hdc; join in 2nd ch of turning ch-2; ch 2 (counts as a hdc in next rnd), turn.

Rnd 12 (13–13): Hdc in next 8 hdc, (2 hdc in next hdc, hdc in next 9 hdc) 14 times; 2 hdc in next hdc; join in 2nd ch of turning ch-2: 176 (192–192); ch 2 (counts as a hdc in next rnd), turn.

Rnd 13 (14–14): Hdc in each hdc; ch 2, turn.

Rep Rnd 13 (14–14) until bonnet measures 5″ (5½″–5½″) from top. Finish off and weave in all ends.

Assembling

With wrong sides tog, pin border to crown, distributing fullness evenly. Sew pieces tog with overcast st in same manner as squares were joined.

Edging

Hold bonnet upside-down with right side of back facing you; join orange at center back edge. Work two rnds of sc around bonnet, working 3 sc in each corner st on each rnd. Finish off.

Rnd 3: Join brown in same st as joining of prev rnd; ch 1, sc in same st, sc in each sc to center sc of right front corner; sc in center sc, ch 51, sc in 2nd ch from hook and in each rem ch: tie made; sc in each sc around bonnet to center sc of left front corner; sc in center sc, ch 51, sc in 2nd ch from hook and in each rem ch: tie made; sc in each rem sc; join in beg sc; finish off and weave in ends.

Rainbow Vest

Sizes: 4 (6–8)

Chest widths: 23″ (25″–27″)

Materials: Sport weight yarn, 4 oz (5 oz–6 oz) total of a variety of colors
Size D aluminum crochet hook, or size required for gauge

Gauge: 4-rnd square = 3¼″ × 3¼″

INSTRUCTIONS

Note: Instructions are written for size 4 with changes for sizes 6 and 8 in parentheses.

Following instructions for Traditional Granny Square on page 11, make two 17-rnd (19-rnd, 21-rnd) squares.

Vest Front

Left shoulder strap: Hold one square with right side facing you; join yarn in 3rd ch-1 sp from upper right-hand corner.

Row 1: Ch 3 (counts as a dc), 2 dc in same sp; (ch 1, sk next 3 dc, 3 dc in next ch-1 sp) 2 (3–3) times; ch 4 (counts as a dc and ch 1 on next row), turn.

Row 2: (Sk next 3 dc, 3 dc in next ch-1 sp, ch 1) 2 (3–3) times, dc in 3rd ch of beg ch-3 of prev row; ch 1, turn.

Row 3: Sl st in next ch-1 sp, ch 3 (counts as a dc), 2 dc in same sp; (ch 1, sk next 3 dc, 3 dc in next ch-1 sp) 2 (3–3) times; ch 4 (counts as a dc and ch 1 on next row), turn.

Rep Rows 2 and 3 until strap measures 6″ (6½″–6¾″). Finish off.

Right shoulder strap: Sk 6 (6–8) ch-1 sps to left of left shoulder strap; join yarn in next ch-1 sp. Rep left shoulder strap instructions.

Vest Back

Rep left and right shoulder strap instructions with second square.

Assembling

Hold vest front and back pieces with wrong sides tog. Carefully matching sts, sew sides of squares tog with overcast st. Sew front and back shoulders straps tog in same manner.

Edgings

Note: All edgings are worked in same color.

Neck edging: Hold vest with right side of front facing you; join yarn in same ch-1 sp as last 3-dc group worked of Row 1 of left front strap.

Rnd 1: Ch 1, sc in same sp, * † (sc between next 2 dc) twice; sc in next ch-1 sp †; rep from † to † 6 (6–8) times more; 2 sc in each row across strap; sc in next ch-1 sp; rep from * once more, ending rep without working last sc; join in beg sc.

Rnd 2: Ch 1, sc between 2 sc around; join in beg sc.

Rnd 3: Rep Row 2; finish off and weave in ends.

Armhole edging: Hold vest with right side of front facing you; join yarn in same ch-1 sp as last 3-dc group worked of Row 1 of right shoulder strap (left side of right front shoulder strap).

Rnd 1: Ch 1, sc in same sp, † [(sc between next 2 dc) twice; sc in next ch-1 sp] twice; (sc between next 2 dc) twice †; sc in next ch-2 sp, sc in joining, sc in next ch-2 sp; rep from † to † once; sc in next ch-1 sp, 2 sc in each row across strap; join in beg sc.

Rnds 2 and 3: Rep Rnds 2 and 3 of neck edging. Finish off and weave in ends.

Holding vest with right side of back facing you; join yarn in same ch-1 sp as last 3-dc group worked of Row 1 of left shoulder strap (left side of left back shoulder strap). Rep Rnds 1 through 3 of Armhole Edging.

Bottom edging: Hold vest with right side facing you and bottom edge at top. Join yarn in seam joining at right-hand side.

Rnd 1: Ch 1, sc in same place, * sc in next ch-2 sp, † (sc between next 2 sc) twice, sc in next ch-1 sp †; rep from † to † across vest; sc in ch-2 sp, sc in joining; rep from * once more, ending rep without working last sc; join in beg sc.

Rnd 2: Ch 1, sc between next 2 sc around vest; join in beg sc.

Rnd 3: Ch 3 (counts as a dc), 4 dc in same sc as joining, sk next 2 sc, sl st in next sc, * sk next 2 sc, 5 dc in next sc; sk next 2 sc, sl st in next sc, sk next 2 sc; rep from * around vest, adjusting sts slightly so that last rep ends with last sl st worked in 3rd ch of beg ch-3.

Sunburst Jumper

Size: Finished Jumper Waist Width = 21″

Finished Jumper Length from shoulder to 1″ above knee = 24″

Materials: Sport weight yarn: 5½ oz dark blue (not including Granny Squares)

For Granny Squares only: Sport weight yarn: ½ oz each of light blue, medium blue, dark blue, light green and turquoise; ¼ oz of medium green and dark green

Size 1 steel crochet hook, or size required for gauge; and two ½″ buttons.

Gauge: 6 sc = 1″; 6 rows = 1″
Sunburst Motif = 3″

INSTRUCTIONS

Referring to chart A for colors of each rnd, make 7 of each of Square A and B.

Chart A

	Square A	Square B
Rnds 1 through 4	Light Green	Light Blue
Rnd 5	Turquoise	Dark Green
Rnd 6	Dark Blue	Turquoise
Rnd 7	Light Blue	Light Green
Rnd 8	Green	Medium Blue

With first color, ch 4, join to form a ring.

Rnd 1: Ch 1, 6 sc in ring; join in first sc: 6 sc.

Rnd 2: Ch 1, 2 sc in each sc; join in first sc: 12 sc.

Rnd 3: Rep Rnd 2: 24 sc.

Rnd 4: Join new color in any sc; ch 3 (counts as a dc), YO, insert hook in same sc as joining, YO and draw through: 3 lps on hook; YO and draw through all 3 lps on hook: dc-group made; ch 2, sk next sc, YO, insert hook in next sc, YO and draw through: 3 lps on hook; YO and draw through 2 lps on hook; YO, insert hook in same sc, YO and draw through: 4 lps on hook; YO and draw through all 4 lps on hook: dc-group made; * ch 2, sk next sc, in next sc work dc-group; rep from * 9 times more; ch 2; join in top of beg dc-group: 12 dc-groups; finish off.

Rnd 5: Join new color in any ch-2 sp; working over same sp, YO, insert hook in skipped sc of prev rnd, YO and draw up a lp to working rnd; (YO and draw through 2 lps) twice: long-dc made; working over same sp and in same sc of prev rnd, work 2 long-dc; sc in top of next dc-group, * working over next ch-2 sp and in next skipped sc of prev rnd, work 3 long-dc, sc in top of next dc-group; rep from * 10 times more; join in first long-dc: 36 long-dc; finish off.

Rnd 6: Join new color in any sc; ch 1, sc in same sc; * sc in next 3 long-dc, sc in next sc; rep from * 10 times more; sc in next 3 long-dc; join in first sc: 48 sc; finish off.

Rnd 7: Join new color in any sc; ch 3 (counts as a dc), 2 dc in same sc as joining: corner made; * † hdc in next 2 sc, sc in next 7 sc, hdc in next 2 sc †; 3 dc in next sc: corner made; rep from * 2 times more, then rep from † to † once; join in 3rd ch of beg ch-3; finish off and weave in ends.

Diagram A

Jumper Top (Make 2) | A | B |

Jumper Bottom Front | A | B | A | B | A |

Jumper Bottom Back | B | A | B | A | B |

Joining: Refer to Diagram A for placement of squares. Hold 2 squares with right sides tog. Carefully matching sts, with medium blue, sew with overcast st in both lps of each st, beg and ending in center dc of corner of square. Continue to join squares tog for Jumper Bottom Front and Back.

Jumper Front

On right side, join dark blue in center dc of corner at top right-hand edge of Jumper Bottom Front, ch 1.

Row 1: Sc in same joining st; * † sc in next dc, sc in next 2 hdc, sc in next 7 sc, sc in next 2 hdc, sc in next 2 dc †, sc in seam, sc in next dc; rep from * 3 times more; rep from † to † once: 79 sc; ch 1, turn.

Row 2: Sc in each sc: 79 sc; ch 1, turn.

Row 3: Insert hook in first sc, YO and draw through, insert hook in next sc, YO and draw through: 3 lps on hook; YO and draw through all lps on hook: beg sc dec made; sc in each sc to last 2 sc; (in next sc, YO and draw through) twice: 3 lps on hook; YO and draw through all lps on hook (sc dec made): 77 sc; ch 1, turn.

Row 4: Sc in each sc: 77 sc; ch 1, turn.

Rep Rows 3 and 4, 7 times more. At end of Row 18, there will be 63 sc.

Row 19: Sc in each sc: 63 sc; ch 1, turn.

Rep Row 19 until piece measures 10″ from Row 1; finish off and weave in ends.

Armhole Shaping: On right side, join yarn in 11th sc from right-hand edge, ch 1.

Row 1: Sc in next 43 sc (10 sc on left edge are left unworked): 43 sc; ch 1, turn.

Row 2: In first 2 sc, work beg sc dec, in next 2 sc, work sc dec; sc in each sc to last 4 sc; (in next 2 sc, work sc dec) twice: 39 sc; ch 1, turn.

Rows 3 and 4: Rep Row 2. At end of Row 4, there will be 31 sc.

Row 5: Sc in each sc: 31 sc; ch 1, turn.

Rows 6 and 7: Rep Row 5. At end of Row 7, finish off and weave in ends.

Hold Jumper Top and Jumper Front with right sides tog. With dark blue, sew Jumper Top and Jumper Front tog with overcast st.

Jumper Back

On right side, join dark blue in center dc of corner at top right-hand edge of Jumper Bottom Front, ch 1. Work same as Jumper Front through Armhole Shaping. Sew Jumper Top and Jumper Back tog in same manner as Jumper Front.

With right sides tog and matching side edges, with dark blue, sew Jumper Front and Jumper Back tog at side seams using overcast st in inner lps only (page 10).

Finishing

Bottom Edging: Hold Jumper upside-down. Join dark blue at either side seam, ch 1.

Rnd 1: Sc in seam; * sc in next 2 dc, sc in next 2 hdc, sc in next 7 sc, sc in next 2 hdc, sc in next 2 dc, sc in seam; rep from * 9 times more, omit last sc and join in first sc: 160 sc; ch 1.

Rnd 2: Sc in each sc: 160 sc; ch 1.

Rnd 3: Sl st in first sc; * sk next 2 sc, in next sc, work 5 dc, sk next 2 sc, sl st in next sc: scallop made; rep from * 31 times more; sk next 2 sc, in next sc, work 5 dc, sk next 2 sc; join in beg sl st: 32 scallops; finish off and weave in ends.

Neck and Armhole Edging: On right side, join dark blue at right side seam, ch 1. Work will begin on front of jumper.

Rnd 1: † Sc in next 10 sc, sc in side of next 6 sc rows; sc in seam, sc in next 2 dc, sc in next 2 hdc, sc in next 7 sc, sc in next 2 hdc, sc in next dc, 3 sc in next dc, sc in next dc †; ch 3 (for left buttonhole), sk next 2 hdc and sc; sc in next 6 sc, sc in next 2 hdc, sc in next 2 dc, sc in seam, sc in next 2 dc, sc in next 2 hdc, sc in next 6 sc; ch 3 (for right buttonhole), sk next sc and 2 hdc, sc in next dc, 3 sc in next dc; sc in next dc, sc in next 2 hdc, sc in next 7 sc, sc in next 2 hdc, sc in next 2 dc, sc in seam; sc in side of next 6 sc rows, sc in next 10 sc; rep from † to † once; sc in next 2 hdc, sc in next 7 sc, sc in next 2 hdc, sc in next 2 dc, sc in seam; sc in next 2 dc, sc in next 2 hdc, sc in next 7 hdc, sc in next dc, 3 sc in next dc; sc in next dc, sc in next 2 hdc, sc in next 7 sc, sc in next 2 hdc, sc in next 2 dc, sc in seam; sc in side of next 6 sc rows, sc in next 10 sc; join in first sc: 186 sc and 2 ch-3 sps; ch 1.

Rnd 2: Sc in next 35 sc; 3 sc in next ch-3 sp, sc in next 21 sc; 3 sc in next ch-3 sp, sc in next 129 sc; join in first sc: 192 sc; finish off and weave in ends.

Straps (make 2)

With dark blue, ch 6.

Row 1: Sc in 2nd ch from hook, sc in next 4 chs: 5 sc; ch 1, turn.

Row 2: Sc in each sc: 5 sc; ch 1, turn.

Rep Row 2 until piece measures 11″ long, or desired length.

Finishing: Sew a button on each strap. Sew straps securely to inside of jumper back.

Granny Pullover

Sizes:

Child size	(Small) 4–5	(Medium) 6–8
Garment width around underarms	30″	32½″
Sleeve Length without cuff folded up	17″	18″

Materials: Sport weight yarn, 5 oz white; 1 oz dark rose; ½ oz (60 yds) dark lavendar; ¾ oz (90 yds) lavendar; ½ oz (60 yds) pink; ¾ oz (90 yds) purple; ¾ oz (90 yds) red
Size D (E) aluminum crochet hook, or size required for gauge

Gauge: For Size Small, Granny Square with Size D hook = 3″
For Size Medium, Granny Square with Size E hook = 3¼″

INSTRUCTIONS

Note: Instructions are written for Size Small with changes for Size Medium in parentheses.

Make a total of 40 squares (Traditional Granny Square #1 on page 11) referring to chart A for colors of each rnd. Make four of each Square A through J.

Joining

Refer to Diagram A for placement of squares. Hold 2 squares with wrong sides together. Carefully matching sts, with white, sew with overcast st in inner lps only (see page 10) in each st across, ending in opposite corner of square. Continue to join squares making 4 rows of squares with 5 squares in each row for front. Rep for back. Set pieces aside.

Diagram A

E	A	B	C	I
H	D	E	F	J
B	G	D	H	A
F	I	J	C	G

Chart A

	Rnd 1	Rnd 2	Rnd 3	Rnd 4
Square A	Red	Lavender	Dark Rose	White
Square B	Lavender	Pink	Purple	White
Square C	Dark Rose	Dark Lavender	Dark Rose	White
Square D	Dark Rose	Purple	Pink	White
Square E	Red	Dark Rose	Red	White
Square F	Red	Lavender	Purple	White
Square G	Red	Purple	Dark Lavender	White
Square H	Pink	Dark Rose	Lavender	White
Square I	Dark Rose	Red	Pink	White
Square J	Purple	Dark Rose	Lavender	White

73

First Sleeve

Beg at bottom edge of sleeve, with white and Size D (E) hook, ch 65 (67).

Row 1: Sc in 2nd ch from hook and in each ch: 64 (66) sc; ch 1, turn.

Row 2: Sc in each sc; ch 1, turn.

Rep Row 2 until piece measures 17″ (18″) from beginning; do not finish off. Continue with Back Neck Yoke.

Back Neck Yoke

Sc in next 32 (33) sc; ch 1, turn. Rep until back neck edge measures 12″ from beg of back neck yoke, ending at inside edge (see Diagram B). Do not finish off. Continue with Second Sleeve.

Second Sleeve

Row 1: Ch 33 (34), sc in 2nd ch from hook and in each ch; sc in each sc across back neck yoke: 64 (66) sc; ch 1, turn.

Row 2: Sc in each sc; ch 1, turn. Rep until second sleeve measures 17″ (18″) from beg of sleeve; finish off and weave in ends.

Left Front Neck Yoke

Hold garment with one sleeve at top and one sleeve at bottom with back neck yoke on the right-hand side. Join white at top of sleeve in sc to the left of back neck edge (see Diagram B).

Row 1: Sc in next 32 (33) sc; ch 1, turn.

Row 2: Sc in each sc to last 2 sc; (insert hook in next sc, YO and draw through) twice: 3 lps on hook; YO and draw through all 3 lps: dec made; 31 (32) sc; ch 1, turn.

Row 3: Sc in each sc: 31 (32) sc; ch 1, turn.

Rows 4 through 9: Rep Rows 2 and 3 three times. At end of Row 9: 28 (29) sc.

Row 10: Sc in each sc: 28 (29) sc; ch 1, turn. Rep until front yoke measures 6″ from beg; finish off and weave in ends. (Note: This is center neck front opening).

Right Front Neck Yoke

Hold garment with sleeve at top and sleeve at bottom, and with back neck yoke on the left-hand side. Beg at outside edge of sleeve at bottom, join white in first unused lp of ch-32 (-33) (see Diagram B).

Row 1: Sc in each sc: 32 (33) sc; ch 1, turn.

Rep Rows 2 through 10 of Left Front Neck Yoke until front yoke measures 6″ from beg; finish off and weave in ends.

Finishing

Hold one granny square piece previously assembled with edge that has 5 granny squares going across width and fold in half; pin at fold to mark center. Rep with bottom edge of back

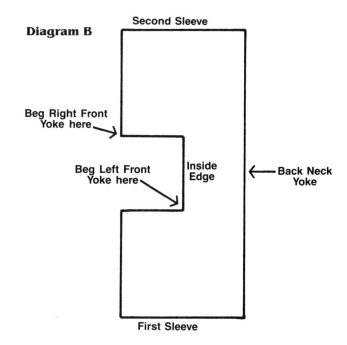

Diagram B

Second Sleeve

Beg Right Front Yoke here

Beg Left Front Yoke here

Inside Edge

Back Neck Yoke

First Sleeve

neck yoke. Placing right sides tog, pin first, matching centers, and sew tog with overcast st. Sew rem granny square piece to front yoke in same manner. Sew underarm and side seams.

Sleeve Edging

Join dark rose at sleeve edge; ch 1, sc in each sc around; join with sl st in first sc; finish off and weave in ends.

Neck Edging

Join dark rose at center back neck edge.

Rnd 1: Ch 1, sc around neck edge to corner of center front opening, adjusting sts as needed to keep work flat; 3 sc in corner st; working down center front opening, sc in each sc to last sc; insert hook in next sc, YO and draw through, insert hook in next sc of opposite center front opening, YO and draw through: 3 lps on hook; YO and draw through all 3 lps: dec made; sc in each sc to corner of center front opening, 3 sc in corner st; sc around neck edge to first sc, adjusting sts as needed to keep work flat; join in first sc.

Rnd 2: Ch 1, sc in each sc around neck edge to corner st; 2 sc in corner st, ch 53, turn, sl st in each ch: tie made; sc in corner st; working down center front opening, sc in each sc to last sc, work dec as in Rnd 1: sc in each sc to corner st; 2 sc in corner st, ch 53, turn, sl st in each ch: tie made; sc in corner st; sc in each sc around neck edge to first sc; join with sl st in first sc; finish off and weave in ends.

Granny's Baby Layette

Tiny granny squares fashion this dainty layette, which includes a jacket, perky bonnet with pompon, snug elf booties, and a beautiful afghan.

Sizes: Instructions are written for one size; change hook size as indicated for size Small (newborn, garment chest 18″); and size Medium (3-months, garment chest size 21″). Afghan is made with larger hook for both sizes.

JACKET, BONNET AND BOOTIES

Materials: Baby weight yarn, 4 oz ombre
Size C aluminum crochet hook for size Small or Size E aluminum crochet hook for size Medium, or size required for gauge
Cardboard

Gauge: One Square with size C hook, for size Small = 1½″
One Square with size E hook, for size Medium = 1¾″

INSTRUCTIONS

Square

Ch 6, join with a sl st to form a ring.

Rnd 1: Sl st in ring, ch 3 (counts as a dc in this and following rnd), 2 dc in ring, (ch 3, 3 dc in ring) 3 times; ch 3; join with a sl st in 3rd ch of beg ch-3.

Rnd 2: Sl st in next 2 dc and in next ch-3 sp; ch 3, in same sp work (dc, ch 3, 2 dc): corner made; * dc in next 3 dc, in next ch-3 sp work (2 dc, ch 3, 2 dc): corner made; rep from

* twice more; dc in next 3 dc; join with a sl st in 3rd ch of beg ch-3; finish off and weave in ends.

Half Square

Ch 6, join with a sl st to form a ring.

Rnd 1: Sl st in ring; ch 5, 3 dc in ring; ch 3: corner sp made; 3 dc in ring, ch 5; join with a sl st in ring, sl st across ring and in next 3 chs of beg ch-5.

Rnd 2: Ch 4, 2 dc in ch sp; dc in next 3 dc; in ch-3 corner sp work (2 dc, ch 3, 2 dc): corner made; dc in next 3 dc, 2 dc in ch-5 sp, ch 4; join with a sl st in last ch of last ch-5 of prev rnd; finish off and weave in ends.

JACKET INSTRUCTIONS

With ombre, make 60 squares.

To join squares, hold two squares with wrong sides tog. Working through inner lps only (see page 10), sew with overcast st, carefully matching sts.

Join in panels as follows: Right Front, 3 sq × 3 sq
Left Front, 3 sq × 3 sq
Back, 6 sq × 3 sq
Sleeves (make two), 4 sq × 3 sq

Yoke

Hold Right Front with right side facing you; join yarn in corner sp of top right-hand square. **Note:** From this point on, work in bl of each st when working a right-side row; when working a wrong-side row, work in fl of each st—this will give the right side of the garment a ridge on every row.

Row 1: * Sc in same sp, sc in next 7 dc, sc in next corner sp;

Fig 1

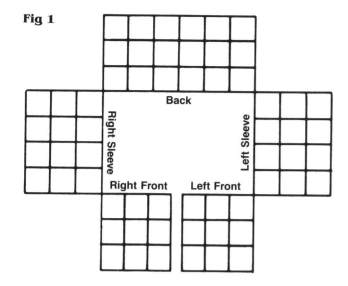

rep from * across rem 2 squares of Right Front, 4 squares of Right Sleeve, 6 squares of Back, 4 squares of Left Sleeve and 3 squares of Left Front (**Fig 1**): 180 sc; ch 1, turn.

Row 2: Sc in each sc to last st of Front, place marker in last st of front and next st; sk the 2 marked sts; sc to last st of Sleeve, place marker in last st of sleeve and in next st; sk the 2 marked sts; sc to last st of Back, place marker in last st of Back and in next st; sk the 2 marked sts; sc to last st of Sleeve, place marker in last st of Sleeve and in next st; sk the 2 marked sts; sc across Front: 172 sc; ch 1, turn.

Note: From now on, move markers up on each row, and sk the 2 marked sts at each of the 4 joining corners on each row.

Rep Row 2, 13 times more. At end of Row 15: 68 sts; do not ch or turn. Do not finish off.

Finishing

With overcast st, sew side and sleeve seams. Continuing with yarn from yoke, ch 45, sl st in 2nd ch from hook and in each rem ch: tie made; sc in top row of yoke; sc in end of 13 rows to first row of yoke, ch 45, sl st in 2nd ch from hook and in each rem ch: tie made; sc in first row of yoke.

Continue with same yarn and working under both lps of each st, sc down entire Left Front of garment, around bottom edge, and up Right Front to beg of yoke; ch 45, sl st in 2nd ch from hook and in each rem ch: tie made; sc in bottom row of yoke; sc in end of 13 rows of yoke; ch 45, sl st in 2nd ch from hook and in each rem ch: tie made; sc in top row of yoke; sc across neckline sts of Front, Sleeve, Back, Sleeve and Front; join with a sl st at base of tie; finish off.

With right side facing you, join yarn with an sc at bottom edge of one sleeve seam; work sc around entire edge, join; finish off. Rep on other sleeve; weave in all yarn ends.

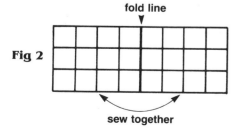

Fig 2

fold line

sew together

BONNET INSTRUCTIONS

With ombre, make 24 Squares.

Join squares as before to make a panel 8 sq × 3 sq. Fold in half and sew back edge (**Fig 2**).

Front Trim

Hold piece with right side facing and long edge at top. Join yarn with an sc in 3rd ch in ch-3 sp of upper right-hand square.

Row 1: Working in bls only, * sc in next 7 dc; sc in first ch of next ch-3 corner sp and in 3rd ch of next ch-3 corner sp; rep from * across, ending sc in next 7 dc, sc in first ch of last ch-3 corner sp; ch 1, turn.

Row 2: Sc in fl of each sc across; ch 1, turn.

Row 3: Sc in bl of each sc across; ch 1, turn.

Row 4: Rep Row 2.

Row 5: Sc in bl of each sc across to last sc, 3 sc in last sc, now working under both lps of each st, sc in end of each Front Trim sc row, 7 sc evenly spaced across each granny square, then 1 sc in end of 5 sc rows of trim; finish off.

Tie

Ch 200, finish off and weave in ends. Starting at left front corner of neck edge, weave tie down through corner, * up in ch-3 sp of first sq, under 4th dc, and down through next ch-3 sp; rep from * across each square, then come up through last corner sp; knot each end of tie.

Pompon

Cut two cardboard circles, each 2″ in diameter. Cut a hole in the center of each circle, approx ½″ diameter. Thread a large-eyed needle with a 72″ length of yarn, doubled. Holding both circles tog, insert needle through center hole, over outside edge, through center again (**Fig 3**), until entire circle is covered. Thread more lengths of yarn as needed.

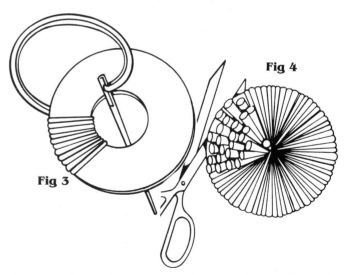

Fig 4

Fig 3

With very sharp scissors, cut yarn between the two circles all around the circumference (**Fig 4**). Using a 12″ strand of yarn doubled, slip yarn between circles, pull up tightly and tie very firmly. Remove cardboards, and fluff out pompon by rolling it between your hands. Trim evenly with scissors. Sew securely to peak of bonnet.

BOOTIES INSTRUCTIONS

With ombre, make 18 squares.

For each bootie, join 9 squares as in **Fig 5**. Then join side A & B to side A & B, side C to C, etc, sewing with overcast st.

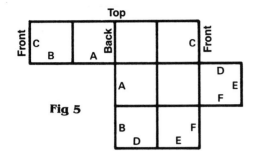

Fig 5

Cuff (work all rnds on right side)

Rnd 1: Join yarn with a sl st at back seam; working in bl only of each st, work 7 sc evenly spaced across each granny square: 28 sc; join with a sl st to first sc.

Rnds 2 through 5: Continuing to work in bl only of each st, sc in each sc; join with a sl st to first sc. At end of Rnd 5, do not ch, finish off. Weave in all ends.

Tie

Ch 120, finish off, weave in ends.

Starting at center front in top row of granny squares, weave tie * down in first ch-3 sp, up and down over 4th dc, up through second ch-3 sp; rep from * across top of bootie. Tie a knot in each end of tie.

Rep for second bootie.

AFGHAN

Size: 36″ × 45″

Materials: Baby weight yarn: 8 oz ombre, 6 oz white
Size E aluminum crochet hook, or size required for gauge

Gauge: One Square = 1¾″

Granny Square Instructions
Same as for Jacket, Bonnet and Booties.

AFGHAN INSTRUCTIONS

With larger hook and ombre, make 225 Squares and 18 Half Squares.

Strips (make 9)

Sew 25 Squares and 2 Half Squares in a strip as shown in **Fig 6**. To sew, hold 2 squares with wrong sides tog, and join with overcast st, working in inner lps only.

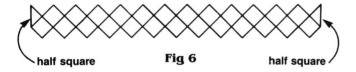

half square   **Fig 6**   half square

Top Chevron Pattern

Hold one strip with right side facing and half squares at sides, in row at top. Work in bls only on right side; on wrong side, work in fls.

Row 1: With white, join yarn with an sc in ch-4 space of Half Square at upper right corner; * sc in next 7 dc, sc in next ch-4 sp; sk corner sp of square below, sc in corner sp of next square, sc in next 7 dc; 3 sc in next corner sp; rep from *, ending by working sc in last corner sp of half square; ch 1, turn.

Row 2: 2 sc in first sc; sc in next 7 sc, sk 2 sc, sc in next 8 sc; 3 sc in corner sc; * sc in next 8 sc, sk 2 sc, sc in next 8 sc; 3 sc in corner sc; rep from *, ending sc in next 7 sc, 2 sc in last sc, ch 1, turn.

Rows 3 through 5: Rep Row 2; at end of Row 5, do not ch; finish off.

Bottom Chevron Pattern

Turn strip upside down and work this chevron pattern along opposite edge. (**Note:** Remember to work in bls only on right-side rows, and to work in fls only on wrong-side rows.)

Row 1: With right side facing, join white with an sc in side corner sp of top right-hand square (**Fig 7**); sc in next 7 dc; * 3 sc in next corner sp, sc in next 7 dc, sc in corner sp; sk corner sp of square below, sc in corner sp of next square; sc in next 7 dc; rep from *, ending 3 sc in corner sp, 1 sc in next 7 dc, sc in corner sp; ch 1, turn.

Fig 7

Row 2: Sk first sc, sc in next 8 sc; * 3 sc in corner sp, sc in next 8 sc; sk 2 sc, sc in next 8 sc; rep from *, ending sc in next 7 sc, sk 1 sc, sc in last sc; ch 1, turn.

Rows 3 and 4: Sk 1 sc, sc in next 8 sc; * 3 sc in next sc, sc in next 8 sc; sk 2 sc, sc in next 8 sc; rep from *, ending sc in next 7 sc, sk 1 sc, sc in last sc; ch 1, turn. At end of Row 4, do not ch; finish off.

Work Top and Bottom Chevron Pattern on each rem strip. With white, sew strips tog, using bls only.

Side Edging

With right side of work facing you, hold piece with one side edge at top; join white with a sl st in first Chevron row at upper right corner.

Row 1: Sc along entire edge of afghan, spacing sts evenly to keep work flat, working in sides of granny squares and sides of Chevron rows; ch 1, turn.

Rows 2 and 3: Working in bls only, sc in each sc, ch 1, turn. At end of Row 3, do not ch, finish off. Rep Edging on opposite side of afghan. Weave in all ends.

Field of Flowers Baby Afghan

Size: About 34½″ × 27″

Materials: Sport weight yarn, 5 oz white; 6 oz colors of your choice
Size D aluminum crochet hook, or size required for gauge

Gauge: 4-rnd square = 3¼″ × 3¼″

INSTRUCTIONS

Referring to Traditional Granny Square #1 on page 11, make 63 four-rnd squares working Rnds 1 through 3 with colors of your choice and Rnd 4 with white.

Assembling

Join squares in 9 rows of 7 squares. To join squares, hold two squares with right sides tog. Carefully matching sts on both squares and with white, sew with overcast st in inner lps (see page 10) only across side, beg and ending with one corner st. Join squares in rows; then sew rows tog in same manner, being sure that all four-corner junctions are firmly joined.

Edging

With right side of afghan facing you, join white in ch-2 sp of upper right-hand corner.

Rnd 1: Ch 3, 4 dc in same sp; ch 1, * † (sk next 3 dc, 3 dc in next ch-1 sp, ch 1) 3 times; (3 dc in next ch-2 sp) twice †; rep from † to † 5 times more; (sk next 3 dc, 3 dc in next ch-1 sp, ch 1) 3 times; sk next 3 dc, 5 dc in next ch-2 corner sp; rep from † to † 8 times; (sk next 3 dc, 3 dc in next ch-1 sp, ch 1) 3 times; sk next 3 dc, 5 dc in next ch-2 corner sp; rep from * once more, ending rep without working last 5 dc; join in 3rd ch of beg ch-3.

Rnd 2: Sl st in next 2 dc; ch 3 (counts as a dc), 4 dc in same st as last sl st made; * sk next 2 sts, sl st in next st, sk next 2 sts, 5 dc in next st; rep from * around afghan, adjusting sts so that a 5-dc group comes at each rem outer corner. Finish off and weave in ends.

Sweet Child Jacket, Bonnet and Afghan

Size: Newborn to 3 months, garment chest 19″

Materials: Sport weight yarn: 3½ oz yellow, ½ oz white, ¼ oz blue, ¼ oz pink
Size E aluminum crochet hook, or size required for gauge
1 yd each of ¼″ and ⅜″ wide yellow satin ribbon

Gauge: One granny square = 2″
Five 2-dc groups = 2″, 3 rows = 1″

Square

With center color (pink or blue), ch 4, join with a sl st to form a ring.

Rnd 1 (right side): Ch 1, sc in ring; * ch 3, sc in ring; rep from * 6 times more; ch 3; join with a sl st in beg sc: 8 ch-3 sps. Finish off center color.

Rnd 2: With right side facing you, join white with a sl st in any ch-3 sp; ch 3 (counts as a dc in this and following rnd), in same sp work (dc, ch 1, 2 dc): corner made; * 2 dc in next ch-3 sp, in next ch-3 sp work (2 dc, ch 1, 2 dc): corner made; rep from * twice more; 2 dc in next ch-3 sp; join with a sl st in 3rd ch of beg ch-3; finish off.

Rnd 3: With right side facing you, join yellow with a sl st in any ch-1 sp; ch 3, in same sp work (2 dc, ch 3, 3 dc): corner made; * (2 dc between next two 2-dc groups) twice; in next ch-1 corner sp work (3 dc, ch 3, 3 dc): corner made; rep from * twice more; (2 dc between next two 2-dc groups) twice; join with a sl st in 3rd ch of beg ch-3; finish off.

Pattern Stitch

Note: Pattern st begins by working foundation row across edge of joined granny squares. Join yarn with a sl st in upper right-hand corner.

Foundation row (right side): Ch 3 (counts as a dc), dc in same sp; 2 dc in each sp across (including sp on each side of joinings); ch 3, turn.

Row 1: 2 dc in each sp, ending dc in sp between last 2 sts (dc and ch-3); ch 3, turn.

Row 2: Dc in first sp (between first dc and next 2-dc group), 2 dc in each sp, ending 2 dc in sp under turning ch; ch 3, turn.

Rep Rows 1 and 2 for patt st.

JACKET INSTRUCTIONS
Body

Following instructions for Granny Squares, make 5 squares with blue centers and 5 squares with pink centers (10 squares total), then join squares into a row using overcast st, alternating the pink and blue center squares.

Beg Pattern St: With right side facing you, hold joined squares with long edge at top and pink center square to your right. Join yellow with a sl st in upper right-hand corner sp.

Work Foundation Row of Patt St: 50, 2-dc groups.

Rep Rows 1 and 2 of Patt St until jacket measures about 5½" from bottom edge, ending by working Row 1 (wrong side row).

Shape Right Front

Row 1: Dc in first sp, 2 dc in next 10 sps, leave rem sps unworked: 11, 2-dc groups; ch 3, turn.

Row 2: 2 dc in each sp, ending with a dc in top of ch-3 (instead of dc in sp between last 2 sts); ch 3, turn.

Row 3: Sk first 2-dc group, 2 dc in each sp across, ending 2 dc in sp under turning ch: 10, 2-dc groups; ch 3, turn.

Rows 4 through 9: Rep Rows 2 and 3, 3 times. At end of Row 9: 7, 2-dc groups. Finish off.

Shape Back

Sk 2 sps from right front shaping just completed (for underarm), join yellow with a sl st in next sp.

Row 1: Ch 3, dc in same sp, 2 dc in next 23 sps, leave rem sps unworked: 24, 2-dc groups; ch 3, turn.

Rows 2 through 9: Rep Rows 1 and 2 of Patt St, 4 times. Finish off.

Shape Left Front

Sk 2 sps from back shaping just completed (for underarm), join yellow with a sl st in next sp.

Row 1: Ch 3, dc in same sp, 2 dc in each sp across, ending 2 dc in sp under turning ch: 11, 2-dc groups; ch 3, turn.

Row 2: 2 dc in each sp, ending dc in sp between last 2 sts; ch 3, turn.

Row 3: Dc in first sp (between first dc and next 2-dc group), 2 dc in each sp across to last 2-dc group, sk group, dc in top of ch-3; ch 3, turn.

Row 4: Sk first 2-dc group, 2 dc in each sp across, ending dc in sp between last 2 sts; ch 3, turn.

Rows 5 through 9: Rep Rows 3 and 4 twice, then rep Row 3 once more. Finish off.

Sleeves (make 2)

Make 2 granny squares with pink centers and one square with

blue center (3 squares total), then join squares into a row, having blue center square between the pink center squares.

Beg Patt St: With right side facing and long edge at top, join yellow with a sl st in upper right-hand corner sp.

Work Foundation Row of Patt St: 15, 2-dc groups.

Rep Rows 1 and 2 of Patt St until sleeve measures 5¾", ending by working Row 2 (right side row). Finish off.

Finishing

Sew shoulder seams. Sew top edge of sleeves to straight edge of armholes, then sew about ½" on each side of sleeves to straight edge of underarms; sew sleeve seams.

Front, Neck and Bottom Edging

With right side facing you, join yellow with a sl st at either shoulder seam; ch 1, work in sc evenly spaced all around front, neck and bottom edges; join with a sl st in beg sc. Finish off and weave in ends.

Sleeve Edging (make 2)

Starting at underarm seam, work edging around each sleeve edge in same manner as above edging.

Tie

Starting and ending in 9th row down from shoulder seam, weave ¼" ribbon through sps up right front, around neck edge and down left front, leaving equal lengths at each end for ties. Trim ends.

BONNET INSTRUCTIONS

Following instructions for Granny Square, make 3 squares with pink centers and 2 squares with blue centers (5 squares total), then join squares into a row (see instructions for Joining Squares), alternating pink and blue center squares.

Beg Patt St: With right side facing you and long edge of joined squares at top, join yellow with a sl st in upper right-hand corner sp.

Work Foundation Row of Patt St: 25, 2-dc groups.

Rep Rows 1 and 2 of Patt St until bonnet measures 5" from front edge, ending by working Row 1 (wrong side row). Finish off; TURN.

Shape Back

With right side facing, sk first 9 sps, join yellow with a sl st in next sp.

Row 1: Ch 3, dc in same sp, 2 dc in each of next 6 sps, leave rem sps unworked: 7 two-dc groups; ch 3, turn.

Rep Rows 1 and 2 of Patt St until back section measures 3". Finish off.

Finishing

Sew back seams. With right side facing you and neck edge at top, join yellow with a sl st in corner sp. Work neck edging as follows.

Row 1: Ch 3, dc in same sp, 2 dc in each of next 4 sps across square, dc in each row across side, dc in each sp across back section, dc in each row across to square at front, 2 dc in each of next 5 sps; ch 4, turn.

Row 2: Dc in next sp, (ch 1, dc in next sp) 4 times; * ch 1, sk next sp, dc in next sp; rep from * across to 2-dc groups at front; (ch 1, dc in next sp) 4 times, ch 1, dc in sp between last 2 sts; ch 1, turn.

Row 3: 2 sc in each sp across. Do not turn; continue with same yarn and work 3 more sc in corner, then work in sc evenly spaced across front edge (work one sc in each dc and in each joining—do not work sc in sp on each side of joinings), join with a sl st in beg sc. Finish off and weave in ends.

Tie

Weave ⅜″ ribbon through sps around neck edge. Trim ends.

AFGHAN

Size: About 24″ × 30″

Materials: Worsted weight yarn: 10 oz yellow, 3½ oz white, 1 oz blue, 1 oz pink
Size G aluminum crochet hook, or size required for gauge

Gauge: One square = 2¾″

AFGHAN INSTRUCTIONS

Following instructions for Granny Square, make 32 squares with blue centers and 31 squares with pink centers (63 squares total), then following **Fig 1** for placement, join squares tog (see instructions for Joining Squares), sewing squares first into rows, then joining rows tog, being careful that each 4-corner junction is firmly joined.

Edging

With right side facing you, join yellow with a sl st in any outer corner sp.

Fig 1

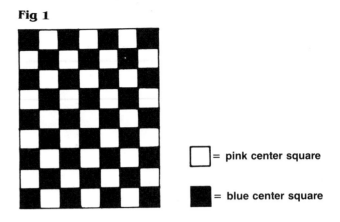

☐ = pink center square

■ = blue center square

Rnd 1: Ch 3, in same sp work (2 dc, ch 3, 3 dc); 2 dc in each sp (including sp on each side of joinings) across to next corner sp, in outer corner sp work (3 dc, ch 3, 3 dc). Work rem sides and corners in same manner, join with a sl st in top of beg ch-3. Do not turn.

Rnd 2: Sl st in next 2 dc and in corner sp, ch 3, work (2 dc, ch 3, 3 dc) in same sp; 2 dc in each sp across to next corner sp, work (3 dc, ch 3, 3 dc) in corner sp. Work rem sides and corners in same manner, join with a sl st in top of beg ch-3.

Rnds 3 through 6: Rep Rnd 2, 4 times more. At end of Rnd 6, finish off and weave in all ends.

Chapter 4
GRANNY FASHIONS

Our granny fashions can take you through your day—there's a warm robe for breakfast; a jacket for cool days, pretty tops for shopping or the office, a bikini for the beach! End your day with a party, and wear the hostess apron.

Pretty in Pink Cardigan

DESIGNED BY JEAN LEINHAUSER

Sizes:	Small	Medium	Large
Body Bust:	32″	34″	36″
Garment Bust:	40″	42″	44″

Size Note: Instructions are the same for all sizes; size difference is achieved by changing hook sizes. Refer to Gauge section below for recommended hook size and specific gauge.

Materials: Worsted weight yarn: 20(23–26) oz or 12(14–15) 50 gr. balls pink; 6(6–6) oz or 4(4–4) 50 gr. balls dk pink Aluminum crochet hook size G(H-I) or size required for gauge 7 wood buttons, 1⅛″ diameter

Gauge: For Small size, with size G hook:
   one granny square = 5″

   For Medium size, with size H hook:
   one granny square = 5¼″

   For Large size, with size I hook:
   one granny square = 5½″

INSTRUCTIONS

Granny Square (make 58)

With dk pink, ch 4, join with a sl st to form a ring.

Rnd 1: Ch 3, 2 dc in ring; (ch 2, 3 dc in ring) 3 times; ch 2, join with a sl st in 3rd ch of beg ch-3.

Rnd 2: Sl st in next 2 dc and in ch-2 sp; ch 3, 2 dc in same sp; ch 2, 3 dc in same sp; * in next ch-2 sp work (3 dc, ch 2, 3 dc); rep from * twice, join with a sl st in 3rd ch of beg ch-3. Finish off dk pink.

Rnd 3: With right side of square facing you, join pink with a sl st in any ch-2 corner sp of prev rnd; in same sp work (ch 3, 2 dc, ch 2, 3 dc); 3 dc between next two 3-dc groups; * in next ch-2 sp work (3 dc, ch 2, 3 dc): corner made; 3 dc between next two 3-dc groups; rep from * twice more; join with a sl st in 3rd ch of beg ch-3.

Rnd 4: Sl st in next 2 dc and in ch-2 corner sp; in same sp work (ch 3, 2 dc, ch 2, 3 dc); work a 3-dc group between each 3-dc along side; * in next ch-2 sp work (3 dc, ch 2, 3 dc):

corner made; 3 dc between each 3-dc along side; rep from * twice; join with a sl st in 3rd ch of beg ch-3.

Rnd 5: Rep Rnd 4. Finish off and weave in all ends.

Assembly

Join squares as shown in **Fig 1**. To join, hold two squares with right sides tog; join with overcast st, working through outer lps only.

Fig 1

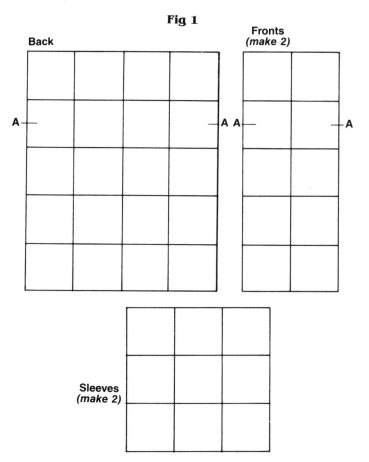

Using same joining method, join Fronts to Back at shoulders, then Fronts to Back at sides, joining only to Point A (**Fig 1**). Set aside.

Sleeves

Join sleeves, in same manner as squares are joined, along 3-square edge. Hold one sleeve with an open edge at top and right side facing you.

Cuff: Rnd 1: Join pink in any joining; ch 3, 2 dc in same place; * (3 dc between next two 3-dc groups) 4 times; 3 dc in joining;

rep from * around, ending last rep without working last 3 dc; join with a sl st in 3rd ch of beg ch-3.

Rnd 2: Sl st in next 2 dc and in sp before next 3-dc group; ch 3, dc in same sp; work 3 dc between each two 3-dc groups around, join with a sl st in 3rd ch of beg ch-3.

Rep Rnd 2 twice more, finish off.

Rep with second cuff.

Setting In Sleeves: Turn body of garment wrong side out; sleeves right side out. Insert sleeve in armhole, with a seam between squares matching shoulder seam. Sew sleeve into armhole, carefully matching sts. Weave in all ends.

Bottom Edge

Row 1: Hold garment with right side facing you, and bottom edge at top. Join pink with an sc in outer corner sp; sc in each dc and each corner sp of each square across; ch 1, turn.

Rows 2 and 3: Sc in each sc, ch 1, turn. At end of Row 3, finish off.

Right Front Band

Hold garment with right side facing you, and center edge of Right Front at top. Join pink with a sl st in 2nd row of sc of Bottom Edge.

Row 1: Ch 3, 2 dc in same place; * 3 dc in corner sp of square, between each two 3-dc groups of square, and in last corner sp of square; rep along front edge to last square, 2 dc in last corner sp of last square; ch 1, turn.

Row 2: Sc in each dc across to beg ch-3 of prev row, sc in top of ch, finish off.

Left Front Band

Hold garment with right side facing you, and center edge of Left Front at top. Join pink with a sl st in corner sp of top right square.

Row 1: Ch 3, dc in same place; 3 dc between each two 3-dc groups and in each corner sp as on Right Front, ending by working 3 dc in 2nd sc row of Bottom edge; ch 1, turn.

Row 2: Sc in each dc across to beg ch of prev row, sc in top of ch, finish off.

Neck Edging

Hold work with wrong side facing, and neck edge at top. Join pink with an sc in upper right-hand corner; sc in each st around; ch 1, turn; sc in each sc, finish off. Weave in all ends. Lightly steam press garment.

Buttons

Sew buttons on first row of Left Front Band, spacing one ½" up from bottom edge, and one ½" down from neck edge. Space other 5 buttons evenly between. Use openings between 3-dc groups on Right Front Band for buttonholes.

Puff Sleeve Sweater
DESIGNED BY JEAN LEINHAUSER

Sizes:	Small	Medium	Large
Body Bust:	32″	34″	36″
Garment Bust:	36″	38″	40″

Size Note: Instructions are the same for all sizes; size difference is achieved by changing hook sizes. Refer to Gauge section below for recommended hook size and specific gauge.

Materials: Worsted-weight yarn: 6(7–8) oz or 4(4–5) 50 gr. balls

Aluminum crochet hook size G (H-I) or size required for gauge

5 wood buttons, ¾″ diameter

Gauge: For Small size, with size G hook: one granny square = 4½″

For Medium size, with H hook: one granny square = 4¾″

For Large size, with I hook, one granny square = 5″

INSTRUCTIONS

Full Square (make 38)

Ch 4, join with a sl st to form a ring.

Rnd 1: Ch 3, 2 dc in ring; (ch 2, 3 dc in ring) 3 times; ch 2, join with a sl st in 3rd ch of beg ch-3.

Rnd 2: Sl st in next 2 dc and in ch-2 sp; in same sp work (ch 3, 2 dc, ch 2, 3 dc); * in next ch-2 sp, work (3 dc, ch 2, 3 dc); rep from * twice, join with a sl st in 3rd ch of beg ch-3.

Rnd 3: Sl st in next 2 dc and in ch-2 sp; in same sp work (ch 3, 2 dc, ch 2, 3 dc); between next two 3-dc groups work 3 dc for side; * (3 dc, ch 2, 3 dc) all in next ch-2 sp for corner; 3 dc between next two 3-dc groups for side; rep from * twice, join with a sl st in 3rd ch of beg ch-3.

Rnd 4: Sl st in next 2 dc and in ch-2 corner sp; in same sp work (ch-3, 2 dc, ch 2, 3 dc); work 3-dc group between each 3-dc group along side; * (3 dc, ch 2, 3 dc) all in next ch-2 sp for corner; 3 dc between each 3-dc group for side; rep from * twice, join with a sl st in 3rd ch of beg ch-3. Finish off and weave in ends.

Half Square (make 2)

Ch 4, join with a sl st to form a ring.

Rnd 1 (right side): Ch 3, 2 dc in ring; ch 2, 3 dc in ring; finish off.

Rnd 2: With right side facing, join yarn with a sl st in 3rd ch of beg ch-3 of prev rnd; ch 3, 2 dc in same sp; in next ch-2 sp work (3 dc, ch 2, 3 dc); sk next 2 dc, 3 dc in next dc; finish off.

Rnd 3: With right side facing, join yarn with a sl st in 3rd ch of beg ch-3 of prev rnd; ch 3, 2 dc in same sp; 3 dc between 3-dc groups to ch-2 sp; in ch-2 sp work (3 dc, ch 2, 3 dc); 3 dc between 3-dc groups to last group, in last dc work 3 dc; finish off.

Rnd 4: Rep Rnd 3. Finish off and weave in all ends.

Assembly

To join, hold two squares with right sides tog, and overcast through outer lps only, taking care to match stitches. Join in this manner following **Fig 1**, making one Back and two Fronts. Then, with right sides tog, join Back to Fronts at shoulder, underarm and side.

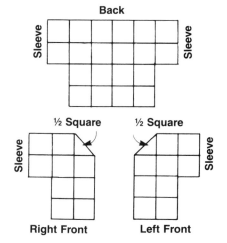

Fig 1

Sleeve Edging

With right side of work facing you, join yarn at underarm seam of one sleeve. * Sc in seam, sc in each dc to next seam; rep from * around; do not join.

Decrease Rnd: * Sc in next sc, sk next sc; rep from * around. Do not join.

Work 3 more rnds, not joining, in sc; finish off. Work second sleeve the same.

Bottom Edging

Hold garment with right side facing you, and bottom edge at top.

Row 1: Join yarn with an sc in outer corner sp of top right square; sc in each dc and in each corner sp across all 8 squares of bottom edge; ch 1, turn.

Row 2: Sc in each sc, ch 1, turn.

Rep Row 2, 3 times. Finish off.

Front Edging

Hold garment with center edge of Right Front at top, with right side facing you.

Foundation Row: Join yarn with an sc in last row of sc of Bottom Edging; sc in next 4 sc rows; sc in each dc, sp and joining of next 4 squares to first half square; across half square, work 3 sc in each dc side, adjusting sts to keep work flat; continue in same manner around neck, across second half square and down left side; ch 1, turn.

Button Band

Sc in each sc to start of half square; ch 1, turn. Work 3 more rows sc on these sts only. Finish off.

Sew buttons to button band, placing top and bottom ones ¼" in from outer edges, and evenly spacing others between.

Buttonhole Band

Hold work with center front of right front at top, wrong side facing. Join yarn in joining before first whole square; sc in each sc to bottom of front, ch 1, turn. Hold band against button band to mark placement of buttonholes. Sc to position for first button, * ch 2, sk 2 sc *; sc to next button, rep from * to *; sc to end; ch 1, turn; sc to end, working 2 sc in each ch-2 sp; ch 1, turn. Sc in each sc to end; finish off.

Weave in all ends, lightly steam press sweater.

Flower Petals Vest

DESIGNED BY JEAN LEINHAUSER

Sizes:	Small	Medium	Large
Body Bust:	32″	34″	36″
Garment Bust:	36″	38″	40″

Size Note: Instructions are the same for all sizes; size difference is achieved by changing hook sizes. Refer to Gauge section below for recommended hook size and specific gauge.

Materials: Worsted-weight yarn: 9(10–11) oz or 6(6–7) 50 gr. balls solid color; 7(8–9) oz or 4(5–6) 50 gr. balls matching ombre

Aluminum crochet hook size G (H-I) or size required for gauge

Gauge: For Small size, with size G hook: one granny square = 4½″

For Medium size, with size H hook: one granny square = 4¾″

For Large size, with size I hook: one granny square = 5″

INSTRUCTIONS

Granny Square (make 40)

With solid color, ch 4, join with a sl st to form a ring.

Rnd 1: Ch 4; (dc in ring, ch 1) 7 times; join with a sl st to 3rd ch of beg ch-4. Do not turn.

Rnd 2: Sl st in next sp; ch 3, work a puff st in same sp, [to make puff st: YO, insert hook in same sp, draw up a lp as high as a dc 3 times; YO, draw through 6 lps, YO and draw through 2 lps: puff st made], ch 1; work (dc, puff st, dc, ch 1) in each sp around; join to top of beg ch-3, finish off and weave in ends.

Rnd 3: With right side facing you, join ombre yarn in any ch-1 sp of prev rnd; ch 3, 2 dc in same sp, ch 2, 3 dc in sp: corner made; * 3 dc in next ch-1 sp, in next ch-1 sp work (3 dc, ch 2, 3 dc): corner made; rep from * twice, 3 dc in next ch-1 sp, join with a sl st in 3rd ch of beg ch-3.

Rnd 4: Sl st in next 2 dc and in ch-3 sp; in same sp work (ch 3, 2 dc, ch 2, 3 dc); * 3 dc between each two 3-dc groups along side; in next ch-2 sp work (3 dc, ch 2, 3 dc): corner made; rep from * twice, work a 3 dc group between each 3-dc group along side; join with a sl st in 3rd ch of beg ch-3. Finish off.

Rnd 5: Join solid color yarn with a sl st in any ch-2 corner sp; 3 sc in same sp; * sc in each dc to corner, 3 sc in corner ch-2 sp; rep from * twice more; sc in each dc, join with a sl st to beg sc. Finish off and weave in ends.

Assembly

To join squares, hold two squares with right sides tog, and overcast with solid color through outer lps only.

Join squares as shown in **Fig 1**.

Fig 1

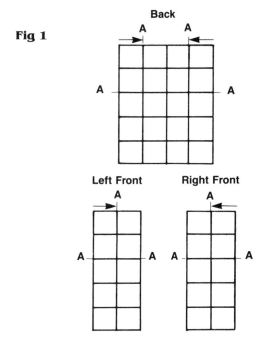

Joining in same manner, sew shoulder and side seams to points A as shown in **Fig 1**.

Armhole Edging

Working with solid color yarn, with right side of work facing you, join yarn with an sc at underarm seam; sc in each dc and each corner sp around, do not join.

Shell Row: * Sc in next sc, sk 1 sc, work shell of 3 dc in next sc, sk 1 sc; rep from * around, join, finish off.

Bottom, Front and Neck Edging

Hold garment with right side facing you, and bottom edge at top. With solid color yarn, join yarn with an sc at center back; sc in each dc and corner sp around entire outer edge of garment, join with a sl st to first sc.

Shell Row: * Sc in next sc, sk 1 sc, work shell of 3 dc in next sc, sk 1 sc; rep from * around, join, finish off.

Weave in all ends. Lightly steam press wrong side of garment.

Sleeveless Shell Top

DESIGNED BY JEAN LEINHAUSER

Sizes:	Small	Medium	Large
Body Bust:	32″	34″	36″
Garment Bust:	36″	38″	40″

Size Note: Instructions are the same for all sizes; size difference is achieved by changing hook sizes. Refer to Gauge section below for recommended hook size and specific gauge.

Materials: Baby-weight pompadour yarn: 12(14–16) oz or 7(8–9) 50 gr. balls
Aluminum crochet hook size E(F-G) or size required for gauge (see gauge note following)

Gauge: For small size, with size E hook: one granny square = 4″ in shell pattern, one shell plus 4 dc = 2″

For medium size, with size F hook: one granny square = 4¼″ in shell pattern, one shell plus 4 dc = 2¼″

For large size, with size G hook: one granny square = 4½″ in shell pattern, one shell plus 4 dc = 2½″

INSTRUCTIONS

Granny Square (make 12)

Ch 5, join to form a ring.

Rnd 1: Ch 3; YO, insert hook in ring and draw up a ½″ lp, YO and draw through 2 lps on hook; YO and draw through 2 lps rem on hook: cluster made; ch 2; * (YO, insert hook in ring and draw up a ½″ lp, YO and draw through 2 lps on hook) twice; YO and draw through 3 lps now on hook: cluster made; ch 2; rep from * 6 times more; join with a sl st in top of beg cluster: 8 clusters.

Rnd 2: Sl st in next ch-2 sp, ch 1; in same sp work (sc, ch 7, sc): corner made; * ch 3, sc in next ch-2 sp, ch 3; in next ch-2 sp work (sc, ch 7, sc): corner made; rep from * twice more; ch 3, sc in last ch-2 sp, ch 3, join with a sl st in beg sc.

Rnd 3: Sl st in first 2 chs of ch-7, and then in ch-7 sp; ch 3, in same sp work (3 dc, ch 2, 7 dc): petal made; * sc in next ch-3 sp, ch 7, sc in next ch-3 sp; in next ch-7 work (7 dc, ch 2, 7 dc): petal made; rep from * twice more; sc in next ch-4 sp, ch 7, sc in next ch-3 sp; in beg ch-7 sp work 3 dc over beg sl sts, join with a sl st in 3rd ch of beg ch-3.

Rnd 4: * Ch 3, in ch-2 sp at tip of petal; work (sc, ch 3, sc); ch 3, sl st in 4th dc from tip; ch 3, sl st in 4th ch of ch-7; ch 3, sl st in 4th dc of next petal; rep from * 3 times, ending last rep by joining with a sl st in first ch of beg ch-3.

Rnd 5: Sl st into next ch-3 sp; ch 3, 3 dc in same sp; * in ch-3 sp at tip of petal work (2 dc, ch 3, 2 dc); work 4 dc in each of next four ch-3 sps; rep from * 3 times more; ending last rep by working 4 dc in each of last three ch-3 sps; join with a sl st in 3rd ch of beg ch-3; finish off and weave in ends.

Assembly

Make two yoke units of six squares each, joined as in **Fig 1**. To join, hold two squares with right sides tog, and overcast working through outer lps only.

Fig 1

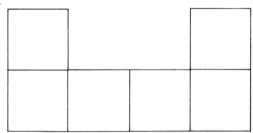

Back

Hold one unit of joined squares with right side facing you, and row of four squares at top.

Row 1: Ch 5; sc in corner sp of first square, then in each dc across square and in corner sp (22 sc); sc in same manner across remaining three squares: 88 sc in all; ch 9, turn.

Row 2: Dc in 4th ch from hook and in next 2 chs; sk 3 chs; in next sc work a shell of (3 dc, ch 3, 3 dc); sk 3 sc, dc in next 4 sc; * sk 3 sc, in next sc work a shell of (3 dc, ch 3, 3 dc); sk 3 sc, dc in next 4 sc; rep from * to last 3 sc of last square; sk 3 sc, shell in next ch, sk 3 chs, dc in last ch. Ch 3, turn.

Row 3: * Shell in center ch-3 of next shell, sk next 3 dc of shell, dc in each of next 4 dc; rep from * across to last shell; shell in center ch-3 of shell, sk next 3 dc of shell, dc in each of next 3 dc and in top of turning ch; ch 3 (counts as a dc in following row), turn.

Row 4: Dc in each of next 3 dc; shell in center ch-3 of next shell, sk next 3 dc of shell, dc in each of next 4 dc; rep from * across to last shell, shell in center ch-3, dc in top of turning ch; ch 3, turn.

Repeat Rows 3 and 4 until shell section measures 15″ long. Finish off.

Front

Work same as back.

Finishing

Place front and back with right sides facing. Sew shoulder and side seams. Turn right side out. Work one row sc around in each armhole opening and around neck. Weave in all ends. Lightly steam press.

Sunflower Sun Top

Sizes: Small (Medium–Large). Garment width around underarms, 31¼″ (35″–37½″).

Materials: Sport weight yarn: white, 3¼ oz; bright yellow, 1½ oz; yellow, 1¼ oz; orange, 1 oz; cream, ½ oz (60 yds) Size D (E–F) aluminum crochet hook, or size required for gauge
Two ⅝″ buttons

Gauge: For size Small, Granny Square = 3⅛″ (size D hook)
For size Medium, Granny Square = 3½″ (size E hook)
For size Large, Granny Square = 3¾″ (size F hook)

INSTRUCTIONS

Using hook giving correct gauge for size desired, make a total of 40 squares (Puff Granny Square on page 12) referring to chart A for colors of each rnd. Make 4 of each Square A through J.

Joining: Refer to Diagram A for placement of squares. Hold 2 squares with wrong sides tog. Carefully matching sts, with white, sew with overcast st in inner lps only (see page 10) in each st across, ending in opposite corner of square. Continue to join squares making 4 rows of squares with 5 squares in each row for front; finish off and weave in ends. Rep for back.

Chart A

	Rnd 1	Rnd 2	Rnd 3	Rnd 4
Square A	bright yellow	cream	orange	white
Square B	yellow	orange	bright yellow	white
Square C	cream	orange	bright yellow	white
Square D	cream	bright yellow	yellow	white
Square E	bright yellow	yellow	orange	white
Square F	orange	cream	bright yellow	white
Square G	orange	bright yellow	yellow	white
Square H	yellow	orange	yellow	white
Square I	yellow	cream	bright yellow	white
Square J	cream	yellow	bright yellow	white

Diagram A

A	B	I	C	J
D	E	F	G	B
C	H	A	I	F
H	J	G	E	D

Hold front and back with wrong sides tog and sew tog at side seams in same manner as joining squares; finish off and weave in ends.

Top Edging

On right side of top edge of camisole, and at either side seam, join white in ch-1 corner sp of granny square to the left of side seam; ch 1.

Rnd 1: * Sc in next 3 trc, (sc in next ch-1 sp, sc in next 2 dc) 3 times, sc in next ch-1 sp, sc in next 3 trc; sc in next 2 ch-1 corner sps; rep from * 9 times more; join in first sc: 180 sc; ch 1.

Rnd 2: Sc in each sc; join in first sc: 180 sc, ch 1.

Rnd 3: * Sk next 2 sc, 5 dc in next sc, sk next 2 sc, sl st in next sc: shell made; rep from * 31 times more; join in beg ch-1: 32 shells; finish off and weave in ends.

Bottom Edging

On right side of bottom edge of camisole, and at either side seam, join white in ch-1 corner sp of granny square to the left of side seam; ch 1.

Rep Rnds 1 and 2 of Top Edging, omit last ch 1; finish off and weave in ends.

Straps (make 2)

With white, ch 5.

Row 1: Sc in 2nd ch from hook and in next 3 chs: 4 sc; ch 1, turn.

Row 2: Sc in each sc; ch 1, turn.

Row 3: Sc in first sc, ch 2, sk next 2 sc, sc in next sc: 2 sc and ch-2 sp; ch 1, turn.

Row 4: Sc in first sc, in next ch-2 sp, work 2 sc; sc in next sc: 4 sc; ch 1, turn.

Row 5: Sc in each sc: 4 sc; ch 1, turn.

Rep Row 5 until strap measures 16″ long, or desired length; leaving a 10″ yarn end, finish off.

Sew buttons into desired place on front of camisole ⅝″ below top of shell (Rnd 2 of top edging). On wrong side of top back edge, place strap ends (without buttonholes) in desired position ⅝″ below top of shell (Rnd 2 of top edging). (Note: You may wish to try on camisole to check length of straps before sewing strap ends onto camisole.) Sew with overcast st in both lps of strap ends onto wrong side of camisole. Finish off and weave in ends.

Sunflower Bikini and Beach Skirt

Sizes: Bikini, to fit 34″ bust and 36″ hips.

Skirt: One size fits all. Skirt length, 28″, skirt bottom edge width, 56″.

Materials: Sport weight yarn: 8¾ oz white, 7¼ oz bright yellow, 1¼ oz orange, and 1 oz yellow
Size O steel crochet hook, or size required for gauge
2 yds ¼″ swimwear elastic

Gauge: 6 sc = 1″; 6 rows = 1″
Square = 3″

INSTRUCTIONS

Make a total of 50 squares (Puff Granny Square on page 12) for bikini top and bottom and skirt referring to Color Chart for colors of each rnd. Make 4 of each Square A through L, plus one more of each Square E and G.

BIKINI TOP

Referring to Color Chart, use 2 squares each of Square C, H, and J. On right side of Puff Granny Square, join white in any ch-1 corner sp, ch 1.

Color Chart

Square	Rnd 1	Rnd 2	Rnd 3	Rnd 4
A	Orange	White	Yellow	White
B	White	Bright Yellow	Orange	White
C	Bright Yellow	White	Bright Yellow	White
D	Orange	White	Bright Yellow	White
E	White	Yellow	Orange	White
F	Yellow	Orange	Bright Yellow	White
G	Orange	Bright Yellow	Yellow	White
H	Bright Yellow	White	Orange	White
I	Orange	Yellow	Bright Yellow	White
J	Yellow	Orange	Yellow	White
K	White	Orange	Bright Yellow	White
L	Bright Yellow	Orange	Bright Yellow	White

Rnd 5: 3 sc in same ch-1 sp; * † sc in next 3 trc, (sc in next ch-1 sp, sc in next 2 dc) 3 times, sc in next ch-1 sp, sc in next 3 trc †, 3 sc in next ch-1 sp; rep from * twice more; rep from † to † once; join in first sc; finish off and weave in ends.

Rep for 5 rem squares, for a total of 6 squares for bikini top.

Joining: Referring to Diagram A for square placement of Left Bikini Top, hold 2 squares with wrong sides tog. Beg and ending in center sc of 3-sc group in ch-1 corner sp of Rnd 5 and carefully matching sts, with white, sew with overcast st in inner lps only (see page 10) in each sc across. In same manner, sew one more square onto the joined square referring to Diagram A for square placement. Refer to Diagram A and in same manner, sew center seam of bikini top. Rep with rem 3 squares of bikini top for Right Bikini Top (see Diagram B).

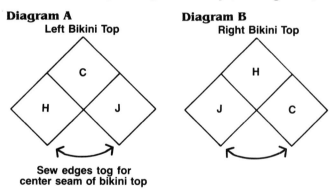

Diagram A
Left Bikini Top

Diagram B
Right Bikini Top

Sew edges tog for
center seam of bikini top

Edging and Ties

Hold Right Bikini Top upside-down with right side facing you and center seam on top. Join bright yellow in center seam, ch 1.

Rnd 1: Sc in seam, sc in next 18 sc, 3 sc in next sc (center sc of 3-sc group); (sc in next 18 sc, sc in seam, sc in next 18 sc, work 3 sc in next sc [center sc of 3-sc group]) twice; sc in next 18 sc; join in first sc: 120 sc, ch 1.

Rnd 2: Sc in next 20 sc; † ch 73 for tie, sc in 2nd ch from hook, sc in each ch, sc in next sc of bikini top, ch 1, turn; sc in each sc of tie, ch 1, turn; sc in each sc of tie, sc in next sc of bikini top: tie made and joined to bikini top †; sc in next 38 sc;

rep from † to † once for neck tie; sc in next 38 sc; 3 sc in next sc for corner; sc in next 18 sc; join in first sc.

Rep for Left Bikini Top through Rnd 1.

Rnd 2: Sc in next 20 sc, 3 sc in next sc for corner; sc in next 38 sc; † ch 73 for tie, sc in 2nd ch from hook, sc in each ch, sc in next sc of bikini top, ch 1, turn; sc in each sc of tie, ch 1, turn; sc in each sc of tie, sc in next sc of bikini top: tie made and joined to bikini top †; sc in next 38 sc; rep from † to † for back tie; sc in next 18 sc; join in first sc.

Hold right and left sides of bikini top with right sides tog. Carefully matching sts, with bright yellow, sew center edges (without ties) in inner lps only (see page 10) for a 1½" seam beginning at bottom edge of bikini top and leaving remainder of center edges open.

BIKINI BOTTOM

Front: With bright yellow, ch 16.

Row 1: Sc in 2nd ch from hook and in each rem ch: 15 sc; ch 1, turn.

Rows 2 through 10: Sc in each sc: 15 sc; ch 1, turn.

Rows 11 through 36: 2 sc in first sc, sc in each sc; ch 1, turn. At end of Row 36, omit last ch-1; do not turn: 41 sc.

Row 37: Ch 27 for leg opening, sc in 2nd ch from hook and in each rem ch; sc in each sc: 67 sc.

Row 38: Ch 27 for leg opening, sc in 2nd ch from hook and in each rem ch; sc in each sc: 93 sc; ch 1, turn.

Row 39: Sc in each sc: 93 sc; ch 1, turn.

Rows 40 through 51: Rep Row 39. At end of Row 51, omit last ch 1; finish off and weave in ends.

Diagram C **Bikini Bottom Front**

K	J	L	B	A

Joining: Referring to Diagram C for placement of squares for Bikini Front, hold 2 squares with wrong sides tog. Carefully matching sts, with white, sew with overcast st in inner

94

lps only (see page 10) in each st across, ending in opposite corner of square. Continue to join squares tog making a long strip of 5 squares.

With right sides tog and matching top edges, place long strip of granny squares on top of bikini bottom. Carefully matching sts, with bright yellow, sew in inner lps only (see page 10) in each st across.

Back

With bright yellow, ch 16.

Row 1: Sc in 2nd ch from hook and in each rem ch: 15 sc; ch 1, turn.

Rows 2 and 3: Sc in each sc: 15 sc; ch 1, turn.

Row 4: 2 sc in first sc, sc in each sc to last sc, 2 sc in last sc: 17 sc; ch 1, turn.

Rows 5 through 42: Rep Row 4. At end of Row 42, omit last ch 1; finish off and weave in ends.

Row 43: Sc in each sc: 93 sc; ch 1, turn.

Rows 44 through 55: Rep Row 43. At end of Row 55, omit ch 1; finish off and weave in ends.

Joining: Sew 5 squares into a long strip in same manner as front of bikini bottom (see Diagram D).

Diagram D   **Bikini Bottom Back**

F	K	G	E	D

Sew long strip of granny squares onto bikini bottom in same manner as front.

Hold right sides tog of front and back bikini pieces. With bright yellow, sew side seams in inner lps only, carefully matching sts. Sew crotch seam in same manner.

Edging

On right side, join bright yellow at crotch seam of leg opening, ch 1.

Rnds 1 through 6: Sc in each sc around; ch 1, join in first sc. At end of Row 6, omit last ch 1; finish off and weave in ends.

Rep for rem leg opening.

On right side, join bright yellow at side seam of upper edge of bikini bottom, ch 1.

Rnd 1: Sc in seam, * sc in next 3 trc, (sc in next ch-1 sp, sc in next 2 dc) 3 times, sc in next ch-1 sp, sc in next 3 trc, sc in next ch-1 corner sp, sc in seam, sc in next ch-1 corner sp; rep from * 9 times more, omit last sc; join in first sc: 191 sc; ch 1.

Rnds 2 through 6: Sc in each sc: 191 sc; ch 1. At end of Rnd 6, omit ch 1; finish off and weave in ends.

Finishing

Fold last 3 rows of sc around upper bikini edge to inside of bikini bottom. On wrong side, sew edge into place to form a casing for elastic, leaving a 1½″ opening to insert elastic. Cut a piece of elastic to fit waist, and insert elastic in casing. Lap elastic ½″ over at each end and stitch securely. Sew opening in casing closed.

Cut a piece of elastic to fit each leg, and rep same as upper bikini edge for leg openings.

BEACH SKIRT

Referring to Diagram E for placement of squares for Skirt Center Front, with white, join 9 squares tog into a long strip in same manner as joining squares for Bikini Bottom Front. Rep for other Skirt Center Front. Set pieces aside.

Diagram E

Skirt Center Front

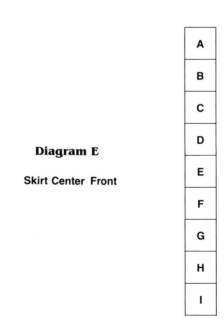

A
B
C
D
E
F
G
H
I

Referring to Diagram F for placement of squares for Skirt Bottom, with white, join 16 squares tog into a long strip in same manner as joining squares for Bikini Bottom Front.

G	B	L	D	E	F	G	L	I	K	J	L	I	K	A	E
															E

On right side of strip, join white in right-hand ch-1 corner sp, ch 1.

Row 1: Ch 3 (counts as first dc), dc in same ch-1 sp, sk next 3 trc; * † (ch 1, 2 dc in next ch-1 sp, sk next 2 dc) 3 times, ch 1, 2 dc in next ch-1 sp, ch 1, sk next 3 trc, 2 dc in next ch-1 corner sp †; ch 1, 2 dc in next ch-1 corner sp; rep from * 14 times more; rep from † to † once: 96, 2-dc groups and 95 ch-1 sps.

Row 2: Ch 4 (counts as ch-4 corner sp); * sk next 2 dc, 2 dc in next ch-1 sp; rep from * 94 times more; ch 1, dc in 3rd ch of beg ch-3 (ch-4 corner sp made: 95, 2-dc groups, 94 ch-1 sps, and 2 ch-4 corner sps).

Row 3: Ch 3 (counts as first dc), dc in same ch-4 corner sp: beg 2-dc group made; * ch 1, sk next 2 dc, 2 dc in next ch-1 sp; rep from * 93 times more; ch 1, 2 dc in next ch-4 corner sp: 96, 2-dc groups and 95 ch-1 sps.

Rep Rows 2 and 3 until piece measures same length as the joined granny squares for the Skirt Center Front.

In same manner as joining squares for Bikini Bottom Front, sew Skirt Center Front to each side of skirt, beg by carefully matching sts of granny square on lower edge of skirt and bottom granny square on Skirt Center Front. Continue to sew rem squares evenly to side of skirt.

Skirt Edging

On right side, join white in top left-hand side of skirt in ch-1 corner sp of granny square.

Row 1: Ch 3 (counts as first dc), dc in same ch-1 corner sp;
ch 1, sk next 3 trc; † (ch 1, 2 dc in next ch-1 sp, sk next 2 dc) 3 times, ch 1, 2 dc in next ch-1 sp, ch 1, sk next 3 trc, 2 dc in next ch-1 corner sp; ch 1, 2 dc in next ch-1 corner sp †; rep from † to † 7 times more; (ch 1, 2 dc in next ch-1 sp, sk next 2 dc) 3 times, ch 1, 2 dc in next ch-1 sp, ch 1, sk next 3 trc; in next ch-1 corner sp, work (2 dc, ch 1, 2 dc, ch 1, 2 dc), sk next 3 trc; rep from † to † 16 times; (ch 1, 2 dc in next ch-1 sp, sk next 2 dc) 3 times, ch 1, 2 dc in next ch-1 sp, ch 1, sk next 3 trc, in next ch-1 corner sp, work (2 dc, ch 1, 2 dc, ch 1, 2 dc), sk next 3 trc; rep from † to † 8 times; (ch 1, 2 dc in next ch-1 sp, sk next 2 dc) 3 times, ch 1, 2 dc in next ch-1 sp, ch 1, sk next 3 trc, 2 dc in next ch-1 corner sp; finish off white.

On right side, join bright yellow in top left-hand side of skirt in 3rd ch of beg ch-3.

Row 2: Sk next dc; * in next ch-1 sp, work 5 dc, sk next 2 dc, sl st in next ch-1 sp; rep from * down skirt center front edge, bottom skirt edge, and up rem skirt center edge, ending with sl st in last dc; finish off and weave in ends.

Waist Tie

With bright yellow, ch 4.

Row 1: Sc in 2nd ch from hook and in each rem ch: 3 sc; ch 1, turn.

Row 2: Sc in each sc: 3 sc; ch 1, turn.

Rep Row 2 until tie measures 48″, or desired length; finish off and weave in ends.

Weave Waist Tie through ch-1 sps in top edge of skirt.

Rainbow Granny Jacket

Sizes: Small (Medium–Large). Garment width around underarms, 40″ (44″–46″).

Materials: Sport weight yarn: 13½ oz in purple for small size (14 oz for medium and large), one oz in lavender for all sizes, and scrap sport weight yarn in a variety of bright colors, not including purple (for granny squares)
Size E aluminum crochet hook for small size (Size F for medium–Size G for large), or size required for gauge
Six ⅝″ buttons
2 beads for neck tie ends (optional).

Gauge: For Size Small, Granny Square = 5″ (Size E hook)
For Size Medium, Granny Square = 5½″ (Size F hook)
For Size Large, Granny Square = 5¾″ (Size G hook)

INSTRUCTIONS

Using hook giving correct gauge for size desired, make 24 squares (6-rnd Traditional Granny Square #1 on page 11) using scrap yarn in bright colors (do not use purple).

Note: If desired, you may work 2 rnds or more of the same color. If continuing with same color for next rnd, do not finish off and proceed as follows: sl st in next 2 dc and into next ch-2 sp.

Yoke

Refer to Diagram A for arranging squares of yoke. Hold 2 squares with wrong sides tog. Carefully matching sts, with purple, sew with overcast st in inner lps only (page 10) in each st across, ending in opposite corner of square. Continue to join squares tog, leaving squares unjoined at center front as indicated, for front opening.

Back

With right side of back yoke facing you, join purple in right-hand corner sp.

Row 1: Ch 3 (counts as first dc), in same sp, work 2 dc, ch 1; * (sk next 3 dc, 3 dc in next ch-1 sp, ch 1) 5 times; sk next corner sp, 3 dc in seam, ch 1, sk next corner sp; rep from * 3 times more, ending with 3 dc in last ch-2 corner sp: 25, 3-dc groups; ch 4 (counts as corner sp in following row), turn.

Row 2: * Sk next 3 dc, 3 dc in next ch-1 sp, ch 1; rep from * 23 times more; dc in last dc (ch-4 corner sp made): 24, 3-dc groups; ch 3 (counts as first dc in following row), turn.

Diagram A

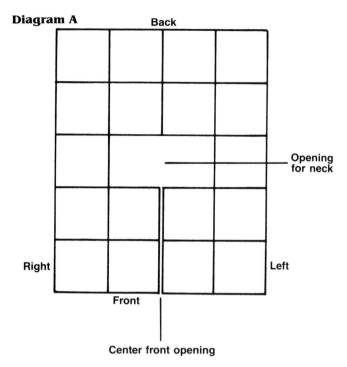

Back

Opening for neck

Right

Left

Front

Center front opening

Row 3: 2 dc in ch-4 corner sp, ch 1; * sk next 3 dc, 3 dc in next ch-1 sp, ch 1; rep from * 22 times more; 3 dc in next ch-4 corner sp: 25, 3-dc groups; ch 4 (counts as corner sp in following row), turn.

Rep Rows 2 and 3 until piece measures 20″ from Row 1 of Back, or desired length; at end of last row, omit last ch 3 (or ch 4); finish off and weave in ends.

Right Front

With right side of front facing, join purple in right-hand corner sp of right-hand side of yoke.

Row 1: Ch 3 (counts as first dc), in same sp, work 2 dc, ch 1; (sk next 3 dc, 3 dc in next ch 1 sp, ch 1) 5 times; 3 dc in seam, ch 1; (3 dc in next ch-1 sp, ch 1) 5 times, 3 dc in last ch-2 corner sp: 13, 3-dc groups; ch 4 (counts as corner sp for following row), turn.

Row 2: * Sk next 3 dc, 3 dc in next ch-1 sp, ch 1; rep from * 11 times more; dc in last dc (ch-4 corner sp made): 12, 3-dc groups; ch 3 (counts as first dc in following row) turn.

Row 3: 2 dc in ch-4 corner sp, ch 1; * sk next 3 dc, 3 dc in next ch-1 sp, ch 1; rep from * 10 times more; 3 dc in next ch-4 corner sp: 13, 3-dc groups; ch 4 (counts as corner sp in following row), turn.

Rep Rows 2 and 3 until piece measures 20″ from Row 1 of Right Front, or desired length; at end of last row, omit last ch 3 (or ch 4); finish off and weave in ends.

Left Front

Work same as Right Front.

Sleeve

Sew 3 granny squares into one long strip in same manner as yoke. With right side facing, join purple in right-hand corner sp.

Row 1: Ch 3 (counts as first dc), in same sp, work 2 dc, ch 1; * (sk next 3 dc, 3 dc in next ch-1 sp, ch 1) 5 times; 3 dc in seam, ch 1; rep from * once; (3 dc in next ch-1 sp, ch 1) 5

times, 3 dc in last ch-2 corner sp: 19, 3-dc groups; ch 4 (counts as corner sp for following row), turn.

Row 2: * Sk next 3 dc, 3 dc in next ch-1 sp, ch 1; rep from * 17 times more; dc in last dc (ch-4 corner sp made): 18, 3-dc groups; ch 3 (counts as first dc in following row), turn.

Row 3: 2 dc in ch-4 corner sp, ch 1; * sk next 3 dc, 3 dc in next ch-1 sp, ch 1; rep from * 17 times more; 3 dc in next ch-4 corner sp: 19, 3-dc groups; ch 4 (counts as corner sp in following row), turn.

Rep Rows 2 and 3 until piece measures about 7¾″ (8″–8¼″) from Row 1 of Sleeve, ending by working Row 2.

Inc Row 1: 2 dc in same sp, ch 1, in same sp, work 3 dc, ch 1: 2, 3-dc groups made; * sk next 3 dc, 3 dc in next ch-1 sp, ch 1; rep from * 17 times more; 3 dc in next ch-4 corner sp, ch 1, in same sp, work 3 dc (2, 3-dc groups made): 21, 3-dc groups; ch 4 (counts as corner sp in following row), turn.

Inc Row 2: * Sk next 3 dc, 3 dc in next ch-1 sp, ch 1; rep from * 19 times more; dc in last dc (ch-4 corner sp made): 20, 3-dc groups; ch 3 (counts as dc in following row), turn.

Inc Row 3: 2 dc in ch-4 corner sp, ch 1; * sk next 3 dc, 3 dc in next ch-1 sp, ch 1; rep from * 19 times more; 3 dc in next ch-4 corner sp: 21, 3-dc groups; ch 4 (counts as corner sp in following row), turn.

Rep Inc Rows 2 and 3 until piece measures about 10¾″ (11″–11¼″) from Row 1 of Sleeve, ending with Inc Row 2.

Inc Row 4: 2 dc in same sp, ch 1, in same sp, work 3 dc, ch 1: 2, 3-dc groups made; * sk next 3 dc, 3 dc in next ch-1 sp, ch 1; rep from * 19 times more; 3 dc in next ch-4 corner sp, ch 1, in same sp, work 3 dc (2, 3-dc groups made): 23, 3-dc groups; ch 4 (counts as corner sp in following row), turn.

Inc Row 5: * Sk next 3 dc, 3 dc in next ch-1 sp, ch 1; rep from * 21 times more; dc in last dc (ch-4 corner sp made): 22, 3-dc groups; ch 3 (counts as first dc in following row), turn.

Inc Row 6: 2 dc in ch-4 corner sp, ch 1; * sk next 3 dc, 3 dc in next ch-1 sp, ch 1; rep from * 21 times more; 3 dc in next ch-4 corner sp: 23, 3-dc groups; ch 4 (counts as corner sp in following row), turn.

Rep Inc Rows 5 and 6 until piece measures 16″ (17″–17½″) from Row 1 of Sleeve, or 1″ less than desired length of sleeve, ending with Inc Row 5, omit last ch 3; finish off purple.

Rep for other sleeve.

Hold sleeve with wrong side facing you and granny squares at bottom, and place on shoulder edge. With purple, sew sleeve in place. Rep for rem sleeve. Sew underarm and side seams.

Center Front and Bottom Edging

With right side facing you, join purple in corner sp at top of neck edge on left front.

Row 1: Ch 3 (counts as first dc), 2 dc in same sp, ch 1: † sk next 3 dc, 3 dc in next ch-1 sp, ch 1 †; rep from † to † working to corner of center front; in corner sp, work 3 dc, ch 2, 3 dc; rep from † to † along bottom edge to corner of center front; in corner sp, work 3 dc, ch 2, 3 dc; rep from † to † along center front to corner sp at top of neck edge, ending with 3 dc in corner sp; finish off purple.

Row 2: With right side facing you, join lavender in 3rd ch of beg ch-3 at top of neck edge on left front; ch 4 (counts as first dc and ch-1 sp); † sk next 3 dc, 3 dc in next ch-1 sp, ch 1 †; rep from † to † working to corner of center front; in corner ch-2 sp, work 3 dc, ch 2, 3 dc; rep from † to † along bottom edge to corner of center front; in corner ch-2 sp, work 3 dc, ch 2,

98

3 dc; rep from † to † along center front to corner sp at top of neck edge, ch 1, dc in last dc; finish off lavender.

Row 3: Join purple in corner sp at top of neck edge on left front; rep Row 1; finish off purple.

Neck Edging

With right side facing you, join purple in dc at top of neck edge on right front.

Row 1: Ch 1, (in side of next dc, work 2 sc) 3 times; † (sc in next 3 dc, sc in next ch) 5 times, sc in next 3 dc; insert hook in next ch of next corner sp, YO and draw through, insert hook in seam, YO and draw through, insert hook in next ch of next corner sp, YO and draw through (4 lps on hook), YO and draw through all 4 lps on hook: double sc dec made †; rep from † to † once; (sc in next 3 dc, sc in next ch) 5 times, sc in next 3 dc, sc in next ch, sc in seam, sc in next ch; rep from † to † twice; (sc in next 3 dc, sc in next ch) 6 times; (in side of next dc, work 2 sc) 3 times: 158 sc; ch 1, turn.

Row 2: Sc in next 29 sc; in next 3 sc, work double sc dec; sc in next 19 sc, in next 3 sc, work double sc dec; sc in next 45 sc; in next 3 sc, work double sc dec; sc in next 19 sc, in next 3 sc, work double sc dec; sc in next 26 sc: 150 sc; ch 1, turn.

Row 3: Sc in next 26 sc; in next 3 sc, work double sc dec; sc in next 19 sc, in next 3 sc, work double sc dec; sc in next 45 sc; in next 3 sc, work double sc dec, sc in next 19 sc; in next 3 sc, work double sc dec; sc in next 29 sc: 142 sc; ch 1, turn.

Row 4: Sc in next 29 sc; in next 3 sc, work double sc dec; sc in next 17 sc, in next 3 sc, work double sc dec; sc in next 43 sc; in next 3 sc, work double sc dec; sc in next 17 sc; in next 3 sc, work double sc dec; sc in next 24 sc: 134 sc; ch 3 (counts as first dc in following row), turn.

Row 5: Dc in next 23 sc; holding back last lp of each dc on hook, dc in next 2 sc, YO and draw through all 3 lps on hook: dec made; dc in next 16 sc, dec as before over next 2 sc; dc in next 42 sc, dec as before; dc in next 16 sc, dec as before; dc in next 28 sc: 130 dc; ch 3 (counts as a dc in following row), turn.

Row 6: Dc in next 27 dc; in next 2 dc, work dc dec, dc in next 15 dc; in next 2 dc, work dc dec; dc in next 41 dc; in next 2 dc, work dc dec, dc in next 15 dc; in next 2 dc, work dc dec, dc in next 23 dc: 126 dc; finish off purple.

Row 7: With right side facing, join lavendar in last dc worked; ch 1, sc in same dc; * sk next 2 dc, 5 dc in next dc, sk next 2 dc, sc in next dc; rep from * 20 times more; finish off lavender.

Tie

With purple, ch 156; finish off purple. Join lavender in end and sl st in each ch across; finish off and weave in ends. Weave tie through Row 5 of Neck Edging. Optional: If desired, string a bead at each end of tie and make a knot at each end.

Sleeve Edging

With right side of sleeve facing you, join purple in corner sp on right-hand side.

Rnd 1: Ch 3 (counts as first dc), 2 dc in same sp, ch 1; † sk next 3 dc, 3 dc in next ch-1 sp, ch 1 †; rep from † to † 4 times more; * sk next corner sp, 3 dc in seam, ch 1, sk next corner sp; rep from † to † 5 times; rep from * once; join with sl st in 3rd ch of beg ch-3: 18, 3-dc groups.

Rnd 2: Sl st in next 3 dc, sl st in next ch-1 sp, ch 3 (counts as first dc), 2 dc in same sp, ch 1; * sk next 3 dc, 3 dc in next ch-1 sp, ch 1; rep from * 16 times more; join with sl st in 3rd ch of beg ch-3: 18, 3-dc groups; finish off purple.

Rnd 3: Join lavender in any ch-1 sp, ch 1, sc in same ch-1 sp, sk next 3 dc, 5 dc in next ch-1 sp; * sk next 3 dc, sc in next ch-1 sp, sk next 3 dc, 5 dc in next ch-1 sp; rep from * 7 times more; join with sl st in first sc; finish off and weave in ends.

Sew six ⅝″ buttons into place on left front using ch-1 sps on right front as buttonholes.

Hostess Apron

Size: One size fits adult. Skirt length is about 33½".

Materials: Sport weight yarn, 22 oz in black and 17 ozs of scrap yarn in various bright colors. Size F aluminum crochet hook, or size required for gauge.

Gauge: Granny Square = 4½"

INSTRUCTIONS

Make 54 squares (Wagon Wheel Square #3 on page 13). Work Rnds 1 through 3 in one color, Rnds 4 and 5 in another color, and Rnd 6 in black.

SKIRT
Joining

Hold 2 squares with wrong sides together. Carefully matching sts, with black, sew with overcast st in inner lps only (see page 10) in each st across beg and ending in sc worked between 5th and 6th dc of corner sp of Rnd 5. Continue to join squares tog making a long strip of 8 squares.

Section 1

On right side, join black on right-hand side in sc worked between 5th and 6th dc of corner sp of Rnd 5: corner sc in following rows. (Note: All following rows will be worked on right side).

Row 1: Ch 3 (counts as first sc), dc in next 18 sc; * dc in next 19 sc of next granny square; rep from * 6 times more: 152 dc; finish off black.

Row 2: Join bright color in 3rd ch of beg ch-3 of prev row; ch 3 (counts as first dc), dc in each dc: 152 dc; finish off color.

Row 3: Join bright color in 3rd ch of beg ch-3 of prev row; ch 3 (counts as first dc), dc in same ch-3: inc made; dc in next 17 dc, 2 dc in next dc; * dc in next 18 dc, 2 dc in next dc; rep from * 7 times more: 161 dc; finish off color.

Row 4: Join bright color in 3rd ch of beg ch-3 of prev row; ch 3 (counts as first dc), dc in each dc: 161 dc; finish off color.

Row 5: Join black in 3rd ch of beg ch-3 of prev row; ch 3 (counts as first dc); * dc in next 15 dc, 2 dc in next dc; rep from * 9 times more: 171 dc; finish off black.

Section 2

Sew 9 squares tog into a long strip in same manner as before. Hold Section 1 with Row 5 top edge and Section 2 with wrong sides tog. Carefully matching sts, with black, sew with overcast st in inner lps only in each st across of Row 5 of Section 1 and in each st across Section 2, beg and ending in corner sc of each square.

On right side, join black in right-hand corner sc of square of Section 2. Note: All following rows will be worked on right side.

Row 1: Ch 3 (counts as first dc), dc in next 18 sc; * dc in next 19 sc of next granny square; rep from * 7 times more: 171 dc; finish off black.

Row 2: Join bright color in 3rd ch of beg ch-3 of prev row; ch 3 (counts as first dc), dc in each dc: 171 dc; finish off color.

Row 3: Join bright color in 3rd ch of beg ch-3 of prev row; ch 3 (counts as first dc), dc in same ch-3: inc made; dc in next 17 dc, 2 dc in next dc; * dc in next 18 dc, 2 dc in next dc; rep from * 8 times more: 181 dc; finish off color.

Row 4: Join bright color in 3rd ch of beg ch-3 of prev row; ch 3 (counts as first dc), dc in each dc: 181 dc; finish off color.

Row 5: Join black in 3rd ch of beg ch-3 of prev row; ch 3 (counts as first dc), * dc in next 19 dc, 2 dc in next dc; rep from * 8 times more: 190 dc; finish off black.

Section 3

Sew 10 squares together into a long strip and join Section 3 to Section 2 in same manner as Section 2 joined to Section 1.

On right side, join black in right-hand corner sc of square of Section 3. (Note: All following rows will be worked on right side).

Row 1: Ch 3 (counts as first dc), dc in next 18 sc; * dc in next 19 sc of next granny square; rep from * 8 times more: 190 dc; finish off black.

Row 2: Join bright color in 3rd ch of beg ch-3 of prev row: ch 3 (counts as first dc), dc in each dc: 190 dc; finish off color.

Row 3: Join bright color in 3rd ch of beg ch-3 of prev row; ch 3 (counts as first dc), dc in same ch-3: inc made; dc in next 17 dc, 2 dc in next dc; * dc in next 18 dc, 2 dc in next dc; rep from * 9 times more: 201 dc; finish off color.

Row 4: Join bright color in 3rd ch of beg ch-3 of prev row; ch 3 (counts as first dc), dc in each dc: 201 dc; finish off color.

Row 5: Join black in 3rd ch of beg ch-3 of prev row; ch 3 (counts as first dc), dc in next 19 dc; * 2 dc in next dc, dc in next 19 dc; rep from * 7 times more; dc in next 21 dc: 209 dc; finish off black.

Section 4

Sew 11 squares together into a long strip and join Section 4 to Section 3 in same manner as other sections joined.

On right side, join black in right-hand corner sc of square of Section 4. Note: All following rows will be worked on right side.

Row 1: Ch 3 (counts as first dc), dc in next 18 sc; * dc in next 19 sc of next granny square; rep from * 9 times more: 209 dc; finish off black.

Row 2: Join bright color in 3rd ch of beg ch-3 of prev row; ch 3 (counts as first dc), dc in each dc: 209 dc; finish off color.

Row 3: Join bright color in 3rd ch of beg ch-3 of prev row; ch 3 (counts as first dc), dc in same ch-3: inc made; dc in next 17 dc, 2 dc in next dc; * dc in next 18 dc, 2 dc in next dc; rep from * 9 times more: 221 dc; finish off black.

Row 4: Join bright color in 3rd ch of beg ch-3 of prev row; ch 3 (counts as first dc), dc in each dc: 221 dc; finish off color.

Row 5: Join black in 3rd ch of beg ch-3 of prev row; ch 3 (counts as first dc), dc in same ch-3: inc made; dc in next 35 dc, 2 dc in next dc; * dc in next 36 dc, 2 dc in next dc; rep from * 3 times more; dc in next 35 dc, 2 dc in next dc: 228 dc; finish off black.

Section 5

Sew 12 squares tog into a long strip and join Section 5 to Section 4 in same manner as other sections joined. On right side, join black in right-hand corner sc of square of Section 5. (Note: All following rows will be worked on right side).

Row 1: Ch 3 (counts as first dc), dc in next 18 sc; * dc in next 19 sc of next granny square; rep from * 10 times more: 228 dc; finish off black.

Row 2: Join bright color in 3rd ch of beg ch-3 of prev row; ch 3 (counts as first dc), dc in each dc: 228 dc; finish off color.

Row 3: Join bright color in 3rd ch of beg ch-3 of prev row; ch 3 (counts as first dc), dc in same ch-3: inc made; dc in next 17 dc, 2 dc in next dc; * dc in next 18 dc, 2 dc in next dc; rep from * 10 times more: 241 dc; finish off color.

Row 4: Join bright color in 3rd ch of beg ch-3 of prev row; ch 3 (counts as first dc), dc in each dc: 241 dc; finish off color.

Row 5: Join black in 3rd ch of beg ch-3 of prev row; ch 3 (counts as first dc), dc in same ch-3: inc made; dc in each dc to last dc; 2 dc in last dc: 243 dc; finish off.

Skirt Edging

Row 1: On right side, join black in first dc of prev row, ch 3 (counts as first dc), dc in each dc: 243 dc; ch 1, turn.

Row 2: Sc in first dc; * ch 3, sk next 2 dc, sc in next dc; rep from * 80 times more: 81 ch-3 sps; turn.

Row 3: Sl st in ch-3 sp; ch 3 (counts as first dc), 2 dc in same ch-3 sp, (ch 3, sl st in 2nd ch from hook: picot made) 3 times, ch 1, 3 dc in same ch-3 sp; * in next ch-3 sp, work 3 dc, (ch 3, sl st in 2nd ch from hook: picot made) 3 times, ch 1, 3 dc in same ch-3 sp: picot point group made; rep from * 79 times more; join with sl st in 3rd ch of beg ch-3: 81 picot point groups; finish off and weave in ends.

Waist Ties and Waistband

Row 1: With black, ch 50 for waist tie, on right side, join with sl st in corner sc of granny square on right hand side of top edge of skirt; sc in same corner sc, sc in next 18 sc; * dc in next 19 sc of next granny square; rep form * 6 times more; ch 51 for waist tie: 152 sc, ch-50, and ch-51; turn.

Row 2: Sc in 2nd ch from hook and in each rem ch; on wrong side of skirt, sc in each sc across skirt front; sc in each ch: 252 sc; ch 1, turn.

Rows 3 through 5: Sc in each sc: 252 sc; at end of Row 5, finish off and weave in ends.

Bib Front

Sew rem 4 squares tog into larger square of 2 rows of 2 squares in same manner as skirt.

Bib Edging

(Note: Edging is worked on 3 sides only of Bib Front).

Row 1: Join black in any corner sc; ch 3 (counts as first dc); * dc in next 36 dc; 3 dc in next dc to form corner; rep from * once; dc in next 36 dc: 115 dc; finish off black.

Row 2: On right side, join bright color in 3rd ch of beg ch-3 of prev row; work same as Row 1: 115 dc; finish off color.

Row 3: On right side, join black in 3rd ch of beg ch-3 of prev row; work same as Row 1: 115 dc; finish off black.

Sew Bib Front to center of waistband of skirt.

On right side, join black with sl st in sc at end of waist tie, sl st in each sc of waist tie, sl st in each sc of waistband to sc prior to Bib Front, dc in next 37 dc on side edge of Bib Front; ch 50 for neck tie, sl st in each ch; dc in next 37 dc on top edge of Bib Front; ch 50 for neck tie, sl st in each ch; dc in next 37 dc on opposite side of Bib Front, sk next sc of waistband, sl st in each sc of waistband and waist tie; finish off black and weave in ends.

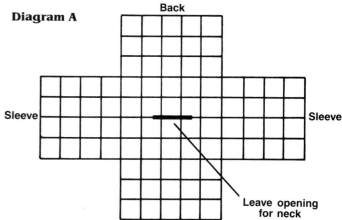

Diagram A

Back

Sleeve

Sleeve

Leave opening
for neck

Wagon Wheel Pullover

Size: Medium (Large). Garment width around underarms, about 45″ (47½″). Note: Garment fits loosely.

Materials: Sport-weight yarn, 13 (15) oz in variety of colors, and 7 (9) oz in black

Size E and F aluminum crochet hook for medium size (Size F and G for large size), or size required for gauge

Gauge: Square with Size F hook = 4½″
Square with Size G hook = 4¾″

INSTRUCTIONS

Make 82 squares (Wagon Wheel Square #3 on page 13). Work Rnds 1 through 3 in same color, Rnds 4 and 5 in same contrasting color, and Rnd 6 in black.

Joining

Refer to Diagram A for arranging squares for pullover. Hold 2 squares with wrong sides tog. Carefully matching sts, with black, sew with overcast st in inner lps only (see page 10) in each st across, ending in opposite corner of square. Continue to join squares tog, leaving squares unjoined as indicated for neck opening. Sew underarm and side seams in same manner as joining squares.

Bottom Ribbing

With black and Size E hook (Size F hook of large size), ch 13.

Row 1: Sc in 2nd ch from hook and in each ch across: 12 sc; ch 1, turn.

Row 2: Sc in back lp only of each sc across: 12 sc; ch 1, turn.

Rep Row 2 until ribbing measures 40″ (42½″) long; ch 1, turn, do not finish off. To join ribbing into one circular piece, insert hook in first ch of opposite end of ribbing, insert hook in first sc of last row worked, YO and draw through: joining sc made; * in next ch of opposite end of ribbing and next sc of last row worked, work joining sc; rep from * 10 times more; finish off and weave in ends.

Place pullover on flat surface and pin bottom edge at sides. Fold pullover matching pins in center, and pin again at sides, dividing bottom edge into fourths. Rep in same manner for bottom ribbing. With right sides together, matching pins, pin ribbing to pullover. Sew ribbing into place.

Sleeve Ribbing

With black and Size E hook (Size F hook for large size), ch 10.

Row 1: Sc in 2nd ch from hook and in each ch across: 9 sc; ch 1, turn.

Row 2: Sc in back lp only of each sc across: 9 sc; ch 1, turn.

Rep Row 2 until sleeve ribbing measures 5½″; ch 1, turn, do not finish off. To join ribbing into one circular piece and sew onto sleeve, refer to instructions for bottom ribbing.

Neck Edging

Join black at shoulder.

Rnd 1: Ch 1, sc in each sc around neck working to keep sts flat.

Rnd 2: Working from left to right, work reverse sc (see page 9) in each sc around; finish off and weave in ends.

Warm-up Lounging Robe

Size: One size fits Misses Size 12 through 16. Garment width around underarms, about 48″, and garment length, about 45″.

Materials: Worsted weight yarn, 30 oz in navy, and 32 oz in variety of blue and green colors
Size E aluminum crochet hook, or size required for gauge
Seven ¾″ buttons

Gauge: 4-rnd square = 4″

INSTRUCTIONS

Make 164 squares (Traditional Granny Square #1 on page 11). Work Rnds 1 through 3 in different colors, and Rnd 4 in navy.

Joining

Refer to Diagram A for arranging squares for robe.

Hold 2 squares with wrong sides tog. Carefully matching sts, with navy, sew with overcast st in inner lps only (see page 10) in each st across, ending in opposite corner of square. Continue to join squares tog leaving squares unjoined at center front and neck as indicated for neck and front opening. Sew side seams and underarms tog in same manner as joining squares.

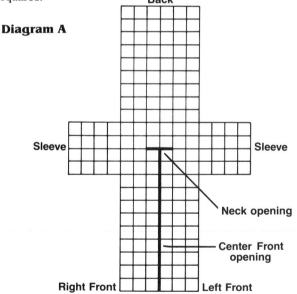

Diagram A

Back

Sleeve

Sleeve

Neck opening

Center Front opening

Right Front

Left Front

Center Front and Bottom Edging

On right side, join navy in ch-2 corner sp of neck edge on right front. Note: Edging will be worked on right side only.

Rnd 1: Working on neck edge, sc in same ch-2 sp, † sc in each st to next ch-2 corner sp, insert hook in ch-2 corner sp of same granny square, YO and draw through, insert hook in ch-2 corner sp of next granny square, YO and draw through:

3 lps on hook; YO and draw through all 3 lps on hook: dec made †; sc in each st of same granny square; rep from † to † once; sc in each st to next ch-2 corner sp, in ch-2 corner sp, work 3 sc for corner; sc in each st to last ch-2 corner sp of left center front; in ch-2 corner sp, work 3 sc for corner; sc in each st to last ch-2 sp of bottom edge of right front; in ch-2 corner sp, work 3 sc for corner; sc in each st to last ch-2 corner sp of right center front edge, in ch-2 corner sp, work 2 sc for corner; join with sl st in first sc; ch 1.

Rnd 2: Sc in each sc to dec from prev row, work dc in next 2 sts; sc in each sc of back neck edge to next dec, work dec in next 2 sts; sc in each sc to center sc of center left front corner, work 3 sc in center sc for corner; sc in each sc to center sc of bottom left front corner, work 3 sc in center sc for corner; sc in each sc to center sc of right front corner, work 3 sc in center sc for corner; sc in each sc to last sc of center right front, work 3 sc in last sc for corner; join with sl st in first sc; ch 1.

Rnd 3: Sc in each sc to dec in prev row, work dec in next 2 sts; sc in each sc of back neck edge to next dec, work dec in next 2 sts; sc in each sc of left front neck edge to center sc of top left front corner, work 3 sc in center sc for corner; sc in each sc of center left front to center sc of bottom left front corner; sc in each sc of bottom edge of robe to center sc of right front corner, work 3 sc in center sc for corner; sc in each sc for next 90 sc (21″ from bottom edge), ch 2, sk next 2 sc, sc in next sc: buttonhole made; * sc in next 9 sc, ch 2, sk next 2 sc, sc in next sc: buttonhole made; rep from * 5 times more; sc in each sc to center sc of right center front corner, work 3 sc in center sc for corner; sc in last sc; join with sl st in first sc; ch 1.

Rnd 4: Sc in each sc to dec on prev row, work dec in next 2 sts; sc in each sc of back neck edge to next dec, work dec in next 2 sts; sc in each sc of left front neck edge to center sc of top left front corner, work 3 sc in center sc for corner; sc in each sc of center left front to center sc of bottom left front corner; sc in each sc to center sc of right front corner of bottom edge of robe, work 3 sc in center sc for corner; sc in next 90 sc, * 2 sc in next ch-2 sp, sc in next 10 sc; rep from * 5 times more, 2 sc in next ch-2 sp; sc in each sc to center sc of right center front corner, sc in next 2 sc; join with sl st in first sc; finish off and weave in ends.

Sleeve Edging

Join navy at underarm seam, ch 1. Note: Edging will be worked on right side only.

Rnd 1: Sc in each st; join with sl st in first sc; ch 1.

Rnds 2 through 6: Rep Rnd 1. At end of Rnd 6, omit ch 1, finish off and weave in ends.

Sew seven ¾″ buttons into place on left front, matching buttonholes on right front.

Chapter 5
USEFUL GRANNYS

This chapter contains projects you'll use for years—placemats, potholders, dish cloths, pin cushions—even a tea cozy!

All of these projects are quick and easy, and make wonderful items for bazaars or craft fairs.

Blue Rhapsody Placemat and Tea Cozy

Size: Place mat: about 12″ × 18″

Tea cozy: about 8½″ high and 18″ around

Materials: Sport weight yarn: 1¼ oz dark blue (not to be used for granny squares), 2 oz medium blue (not to be used for granny squares), 2 oz scrap yarn (for granny squares only) in various blue and turquoise colors, and ¼ oz turquoise

Size O steel crochet hook, or size required for gauge

Gauge: 6 sc = 1″; 6 rows = 1″
        Puff Granny Square = 3″

INSTRUCTIONS

Make 14 squares (Puff Granny Square on page 12) for place mat and cozy.

PLACE MAT
Joining

Hold 2 squares with wrong sides tog. Carefully matching sts, with medium blue, sew with overcast st in inner lps only (see page 10) in each st across, ending in opposite corner of square. Continue to join squares tog making a long strip of 4 squares. Rep for opposite side of place mat.

Hold one strip with right side facing you and long edge at top; join medium blue in ch-1 corner sp of upper right-hand corner, ch 1.

Row 1: Sc in same ch-1 corner sp; * sc in next 3 trc, (sc in next ch-1 sp, sc in next 2 dc) 3 times, sc in next ch-1 sp, sc in next 3 trc, sc in next ch-1 corner sp, sc in ch-1 corner sp of next granny square; rep from * 3 times, omit last sc: 72 sc; ch 1, turn.

Row 2: Sc in each sc: 72 sc; ch 1, turn.

Rep Row 2 until piece measures 12″ from Row 1; leaving a 20″ yarn end for sewing, finish off. With wrong sides tog and carefully matching sts, sew rem strip of 4 squares with overcast st in both lps of place mat and both lps of granny square.

Edging

On right side, join dark blue in top right-hand ch-1 corner sp of place mat, ch 1.

Rnd 1: * † Sc in next 3 trc, (sc in next ch-1 sp, sc in next 2 dc) 3 times, sc in next ch-1 sp, sc in next 3 trc †; sc in next ch-1 corner sp; sc in side of each sc to next ch-1 corner sp of granny square; sc in next ch-1 corner sp of granny square; rep from † to † once; 3 sc in next ch-1 corner sp; (rep from † to † once, sc in next 2 ch-1 corner sps) 3 times; rep from † to † once, 3 sc in next ch-1 corner sp; rep from * once; join in first sc; ch 1.

Rnd 2: Sc in each sc; ch 1.

Rnd 3: Join dark blue in first sc following any 3-sc corner; ch 3 (counts as a dc), 4 dc in same sc as joining; * sk next 2 sc, sl st in next sc, 5 dc in next sc; rep from * around place-mat, adjusting sts slightly so that last rep ends without working last 5 dc; join in 3rd ch of beg ch-3; finish off and weave in ends.

TEA COZY
Joining

Sew 3 squares tog into a long strip in same manner as placement for front of cozy; rep for back of cozy.

Front

On right side, join dark blue in top right-hand ch-1 corner sp of strip, ch 1.

Row 1: Sc in same ch-1 corner sp; * sc in next 3 trc, (sc in next ch-1 sp, sc in next 2 dc) 3 times, sc in next ch-1 sp, sc in next 3 trc, sc in next ch-1 corner sp, sc in ch-1 corner sp of next granny square; rep from * 2 times more, omit last sc: 53 sc; ch 1, turn.

Row 2: Sc in each sc: 53 sc; ch 1, turn.

Rep Row 2 until piece measures about 4″ from Row 1, ending on wrong side; ch 3 (counts as first dc in following row), turn.

Edging

Row 1: Sk first sc, dc in next sc; * ch 2, sk next 2 sc, dc in next 2 sc; rep from * 11 times more; ch 2, sk next 2 sc, 2 dc in next sc: 13 ch-2 sps; ch 1, turn.

Row 2: * Sc in next 2 dc, 2 sc in next ch-2 sps; rep from * 12 times more; sc in next dc, sc in 3rd ch of beg ch-3: 54 sc; ch 1, turn.

Rows 3 and 4: Sc in each sc: 54 sc, ch 1, turn.

Row 5 (right side): Sk first 3 sc, * 5 dc in next sc, sk next 2 sc, sl st in next sc, sk next 2 sc; rep from * 7 times more; 5 dc in next dc, sk next sc, sl st in next sc: 9 scallops; finish off and weave in ends.

Back

Work same as Front.

Finishing

With wrong sides tog and carefully matching sts, sew side seams of front and back tog, beg at bottom edge of cozy and ending at top of granny square. Leave a 4″ opening on each side for spout and handle (Note: You may wish to measure tea pot for placement of opening and opening size). Sew remainder of side seams tog.

Twisted Cord

Step 1: Cut 8 strands of turquoise yarn, each 4 times the cord length (28″).

Step 2: Make a lp at each end of strands, sufficient in size to slip over a door knob or onto a hook.

Step 3: Place one lp on knob or hook.

Step 4: Slip other lp at opposite end of index finger (or several fingers depending on size of lp) or onto a pencil. (Note: For a quicker method, tie this looped end to one beater of an electric mixer.)

Step 5: Holding strands taut, twist strands in one direction until firm and slightly kinky along the entire length. (Note: For quicker method, twist strands with an electric mixer—remember it is better to overbeat than to underbeat.)

Step 6: Keeping strands taut, fold twisted strands over in half, then slip lp off finger(s) or pencil (or beater) and place onto knob or hook with other looped end.

Step 7: Still keeping strands taut, let strands twist tog using the thumb and finger of one hand to guide and smooth out strands as they form into a twisted cord.

Step 8: Knot each end of cord, and cut off excess cording. Trim yarn ends evenly at each end of cord.

Weave Twisted Cord through sps of Row 1 of Edging on Tea Cozy.

Accent Potholders

Size: About 9″ × 9″

Materials: Sport weight 100% cotton yarn, 2 oz black; 1 oz gray; 1 oz off white

Size F aluminum crochet hook, or size required for gauge

Gauge: 3 rnds = 3¾″

INSTRUCTIONS

Following instructions for Wagon Wheel Square #1 on page 13, make 2 squares with Color A—gray, Color B—off white, and Color C—black.

Border

Hold square with right side facing you, join gray with a sl st in trc of any corner.

Rnd 1: Ch 3 (counts as a dc in this and following rnds), in same trc work (trc, dc): corner made; * dc in next 16 dc; in next trc work (dc, trc, dc): corner made; rep from * 3 times more, ending last rep without working last (dc, trc, dc); join in 3rd ch of beg ch-3; finish off.

Rnd 2: Join off white in trc of any corner; ch 3, in same trc work (trc, dc): corner made; * dc in next 18 dc, in next trc work (dc, trc, dc): corner made; rep from * 3 times more, ending last rep without working last (dc, trc, dc); join in 3rd ch of beg ch-3; finish off.

Rnd 3: Join black in trc of any corner; ch 3, in same trc work (trc, dc): corner made; * dc in next 20 dc, in next trc work (dc, trc, dc): corner made; rep from * 3 times more, ending last rep without working last (dc, trc, dc); join in 3rd ch of beg ch-3.

Rnd 4: Sl st in next trc; ch 3, 4 dc in same trc as joining; * sk next 2 dc, sl st in next dc, sk next 2 dc, 5 dc in next dc; rep from * around potholder, adjusting sts slightly so that a 5-dc group is worked in trc of each rem outer corner and patt ends evenly. Finish off and weave in ends.

Wagon Wheel Pillow

Size: To fit a 12″ pillow form

Materials: Sport weight yarn, 3 oz dk blue; 2 oz med blue; 2 oz lt blue

Size D aluminum crochet hook, or size required for gauge

12″ pillow form

Gauge: 6-rnd square = 4″

INSTRUCTIONS

Following instructions for Wagon Wheel Square #1 on page 13, make 18 squares. Make 9 squares with Color A—lt blue, Color B—med blue, and Color C—dk blue. Make 9 squares with Color A—med blue, Color B—lt blue, and Color C—dk blue.

Joining

Join squares into 2 larger squares, each having 3 rows of 3 squares; refer to photo for placement of squares. To join squares, hold two squares with right sides tog. Carefully matching sts on both and with dk blue, sew with overcast st in inner lps (see page 10) only across side, beg and ending with one corner st. Join in rows; then sew rows tog in same manner, being sure that all four-corner junctions are firmly joined.

Assembling

Hold squares with wrong sides tog, carefully matching sts on both pieces. Join dk blue with a sl st in trc in upper right-hand corner; work 3 sc thru same trc as joining and at the same time thru same st on back piece; continuing to work thru same st on both pieces, sc in each dc and 3 sc in each trc around 3 sides of pillow. Insert pillow form. Continue in patt across 4th side; join with a sl st in beg sc.

Edging

Sl st in next sc; ch 3, 4 dc in same sc, * sk 2 sc, sl st in next sc, sk next 2 sc, 5 dc in next sc; rep from * around pillow, adjusting sts slightly so that a 5-dc group comes at center sc of each rem outer corner and patt ends with a sl st in 3rd ch of beg ch-3; finish off and weave in ends.

Strawberries and Cream Placemat

Size: About 13″ × 17″

Materials: Sport weight yarn, 2 oz each of cream, lt rose, and dk rose
Size D aluminum crochet hook, or size required for gauge

Gauge: 6-rnd square = 4″

INSTRUCTIONS

Following instructions for Wagon Wheel Square #1 on page 13, make 12 squares with Color A—cream, Color B—lt rose, and Color C—dk rose.

Joining

Join squares in 3 rows with 4 squares. To join squares, hold two squares with right sides tog. Carefully matching sts on both and with dk rose, sew with overcast st in inner lps (see page 10) only across side, beg and ending with one corner st. Join in rows; then sew rows tog in same manner, being sure that all four-corner junctions are firmly joined.

Edging

Hold placemat with right side facing you; join dk rose with a sl st in center trc of upper right-hand corner; ch 3, 4 dc in same trc as joining; * sk 2 dc, sl st in next dc, sk 2 dc, 5 dc in next dc; rep from * around, adjusting sts slightly so that a 5-dc group is worked in trc of each rem outer corner and patt ends evenly. Finish off and weave in ends.

Pillow of Pinks

Size: To fit a 12″ pillow form

Materials: Sport weight yarn, 2 oz vermillion; 2 oz rose; 1½ oz pink
Size E aluminum crochet hook, or size required for gauge
12″ pillow form

Gauge: One square = 4½″ × 4½″

INSTRUCTIONS

Following instructions for Log Cabin Square on page 12, make 8 squares with Color A—vermillion, Color B—pink, and Color C—rose.

Joining

Join squares into two larger squares, each having 2 rows of 2 squares. To join squares, hold two squares with right sides tog. Carefully matching sts on both squares and with rose, sew with overcast st in inner lps (see page 10) only across side, beg and ending with one corner st. Join squares in rows; then sew rows tog in same manner, being sure that all four-corner junctions are firmly joined.

Square Border

Back: Hold one large square with right side facing you; join vermillion in center sc of 3-sc corner group of upper right-hand outer corner.

Rnd 1: Ch 1, 3 sc in same sc: corner made; * sc in each sc and in each joining across side; 3 sc in center sc of next 3-sc corner group; rep from * twice more; sc in each sc and in each joining across last side; join in beg ch-1.

Rnd 2: Sc in next sc, 3 sc in next sc: corner made; sc in each sc around, working 3 sc in center sc of each 3-sc corner group; join in beg sc; finish off vermillion.

Rnd 3: Join pink in center sc of any 3-sc outer corner group; ch 3, in same sc work (dc, ch 2, 2 dc): corner made; [* ch 1, sk 2 sc, 2 dc in next sc; rep from * to next corner, adjusting sts as you work so that you can sk 2 sc before center sc of next 3-sc corner group; in center sc of next 3-sc corner group, work (2 dc, ch 2, 2 dc)] 4 times, ending last rep without working last (2 dc, ch 2, 2 dc); join in 3rd ch of beg ch-3; finish off pink.

Rnd 4: Join vermillion in ch-2 sp of any corner sp; ch 1, 3 sc in same sp; * sc in each sc and in each ch-1 sp across side, 3 sc in next ch-2 sp; rep from * around; join in first sc; finish off vermillion and weave in ends.

Front: Work same as back piece, but do not finish off at end of Rnd 4.

Assembling

Hold front and back with wrong sides tog and front side facing you; carefully match sts on both pieces. Working through same st on front and back, sl st in next sc, * ch 3, 4 dc in same st, * sk next 2 sc, sl st in next sc, sk next 2 sc, 5 dc in next sc; rep from * around 3 sides of pillow, adjusting sts slightly so that a 5-dc group comes at center sc of each rem outer corner; insert pillow form; continue patt on 4th side; join in 3rd ch of beg ch-3; finish off and weave in ends.

113

Log Cabin Placemat and Napkin

Sizes: Placemat = 12″ × 16″; napkin = 8″ × 8″

Materials: Sport weight yarn, 1½ oz each of pink, rose and vermillion for placemat; 1 oz of pink, ½ oz each of rose and vermillion for napkin

Size D aluminum crochet hook, or size required for gauge

Gauge: One square = 4″ × 4″

PLACEMAT INSTRUCTIONS

Following instructions for Log Cabin Square on page 12 and referring to Diagram A for colors of each rnd, make 12 squares, 6 each of Square A and Square B.

Diagram A

Rnds	Square A	Square B
1 through 7	Pink	Rose
8	Rose	Pink
9	Vermillion	Vermillion
10 and 11	Rose	Pink

Assembling

Join squares in 3 rows of 4 squares, referring to photo for placement of squares. To join squares, hold two squares with right sides tog. Carefully matching sts on both squares and with pink, sew with overcast st in inner lps (see page 10) only across side, beg and ending with one corner st. Join squares in rows; then sew rows tog in same manner, being sure that all four-corner junctions are firmly joined.

Edging

Hold placemat with right side facing you; join vermillion with sl st in center sc of 3-sc corner group of upper right-hand corner.

Rnd 1: Ch 1, 3 sc in same sc: corner made; * sc in each sc and in each joining across side, working 3 sc in center sc of next 3-sc corner group; rep from * twice more; sc in each sc and in each joining across last side; join in first sc.

Rnd 2: Sl st in next sc, ch 3 (counts as a dc), 4 dc in same st as joining, sk next 2 sc, sl st in next sc, sk next 2 sc, * 5 dc in next sc, sk next 2 sc, sl st in next sc, sk next 2 sc; rep from

* around placemat, adjusting sts slightly if necessary to have patt end evenly; join in 3rd ch of beg ch-3. Finish off and weave in ends.

NAPKIN INSTRUCTIONS

Following instructions for Log Cabin Square on page 12, make 4 squares of Square A, referring to Diagram A for colors of each rnd.

Assembling

With dk rose, join squares in 2 rows of 2 squares, in same manner as placemat squares are joined.

Edging

Hold napkin with right side facing you; join pink in center sc of 3-sc corner group of upper right-hand corner.

Rnd 1: Ch 1, 3 sc in same sc: corner made; * sc in each sc and in each joining across side, working 3 sc in center sc of next 3-sc corner; rep from * twice more; sc in each sc and in each joining across side; join in first sc.

Rnd 2: Ch 1, sc in same st as joining, 3 sc in next sc, sc in each sc, working 3 sc in center sc of each rem outer corner; join in beg sc; finish off.

Rnd 3: Join vermillion in center sc on any corner; ch 3 (counts as a dc), in same sc work (dc, ch 2, 2 dc): corner made; * † ch 1, sk 2 sc, 2 dc in next sc †; rep from † to † to next corner, adjusting sts as so that you sk 2 sc before center sc of next 3-sc corner; in center sc of next 3-sc corner work (2 dc, ch 2, 2 dc): corner made; rep from * 3 times more, ending last rep without working last (2 dc, ch 2, 2 dc); join in 3rd ch of beg ch-3; finish off.

Rnd 4: Join pink in any ch-2 corner sp; ch 1, 3 sc in same sp; * sc in each sc and in each ch-1 sp across side; 3 sc in next ch-2 corner sp; rep from * 3 times more, ending last rep without working 3 sc in last ch-2 corner sp; join in first sc.

Rnd 5: Sl st in next sc; 3 sc in next sc: corner made; sc in each sc, working 3 sc in each rem outer corner; join in first sc; finish off.

Rnd 6: Join vermillion in center sc of any 3-sc corner; ch 3 (counts as a dc), 4 dc in same st as joining, sk next 2 sc, sl st in next sc, sk next 2 sc; * 5 dc in next sc, sk next 2 sc, sl st in next sc, sk next 2 sc; rep from * around napkin, adjusting sts slightly to have patt end evenly; join in 3rd ch of beg ch-3; finish off and weave in ends.

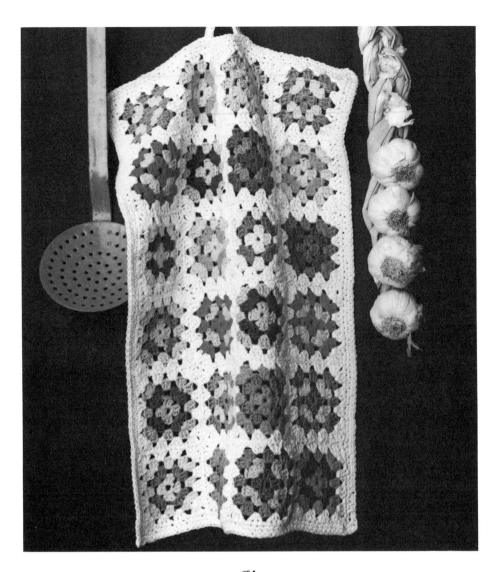

Crocheted Towel

Size: About 13″ × 19″

Materials: 144 yds of white sport weight cotton yarn, remnants of sport weight cotton yarn in different colors
Size E aluminum crochet hook, or size required for gauge

Gauge: 11 sc = 2″; 11 rows = 2″
4-rnd square = 2⅞″

INSTRUCTIONS

Make 24 squares (Traditional Granny Square #1 on page 11). For each square, work Rnds 1 and 3 in same color, Rnd 2 in different color, and Rnd 4 in white. Towel has 6 rows with 4 squares in each row.

Joining

Hold 2 squares with wrong sides tog. Carefully matching sts, sew with overcast st in inner lps only (see page 10) in each st across, ending in opposite corner of square. Continue to join squares tog.

Edging

Rnd 1: Join white in corner st, ch 1 (counts as sc), in same corner st, work 2 sc; * sc in each st across to next corner st, work 3 sc in corner st; rep from * 2 times more, sc in each st across; join with sl st in beg ch-1.

Rnds 2 and 3: Ch 1 (counts as sc), in same st, work 2 sc; * sc in each st across to next corner st, work 3 sc in corner st; rep from * twice more, sc in each st across; join with sl st in beg ch-1; at end of Rnd 3, finish off and weave in ends.

Hanging Loop

Row 1: Ch 21, sc in 2nd ch from hook; sc in each ch across: 20 sc; ch 1, turn.

Rows 2 and 3: Sc in each sc across: 20 sc; ch 1, turn; do not ch 1 at end of Row 3, finish off and weave in ends. Sew ends to center top edge of towel.

Starburst Pin Cushion

Size: About 5¾″ in diameter

Materials: Sport weight yarn in colors of your choice, ½ oz Color A; ¼ oz Color B; ½ oz Color C; 1 oz Color D
Size F aluminum crochet hook, or size required for gauge; polyester fiberfill for stuffing

INSTRUCTIONS

Top

Note: Work with double strand of yarn throughout. With Color A, ch 4, join to form a ring.

Rnd 1: Ch 1, 6 sc in ring; join in first sc: 6 sc.

Rnd 2: Ch 1, 2 sc in each sc; join in first sc: 12 sc.

Rnd 3: Ch 1, * sc in next sc, 2 sc in next sc; rep from * 5 times more; join in first sc: 18 sc.

Rnd 4: Ch 1, * sc in next 2 sc; 2 sc in next sc; rep from * 5 times more; join in first sc: 24 sc.

Rnd 5: Ch 1, * sc in next 2 sc, 2 sc in next sc; rep from * 7 times more; join in first sc: 32 sc; finish off Color A.

Rnd 6: Join Color B at any sc; ch 3 (counts as a dc), hdc in same sc as joining: dc-group made; * ch 2, sk next sc, in next sc work (YO, insert hook in same sc and draw up a lp: 3 lps on hook; YO and draw through 2 lps on hook; YO, insert hook in same sc and draw up a lp: 4 lps on hook; YO and draw through all 4 lps on hook): dc-group made; rep from * 14 times more; ch 2; join in top of beg dc-group: 16 dc-groups; finish off Color B.

Rnd 7: Join Color C in any ch-2 sp; * working over next ch-2 sp, YO and insert hook in skipped sc of prev rnd, YO and draw up a lp to working rnd, (YO and draw through 2 lps) twice: long-dc made; working over same sp and in same sc of prev rnd, work 2 long-dc; sc in top of next dc-group; * working over next ch-2 sp and in next skipped sc of prev rnd, work 3 long-dc; sc in top of next dc-group; rep from * 14 times more; join in first long-dc: 48 long-dc; finish off Color C.

Rnd 8: Join Color D in any sc, ch 1, sc in same sc; * sc in next 3 long-dc, sc in next sc; rep from * 14 times more; sc in next 3 long-dc; join in first sc: 64 sc.

Rnds 9 through 11: Ch 1, sc in each sc: 64 sc. At end of Rnd 11, finish off and weave in ends.

Pin Cushion Bottom

Work same as Pin Cushion Top.

Finishing

With wrong sides tog and using one strand of yarn, carefully matching sts, sew with overcast st through both lps of top and bottom, leaving a 2″ opening. Stuff firmly with polyester fiberfill. Sew opening closed in same manner; finish off and weave in ends.

Shades of Purple
Placemat

Size: About 14″ × 18″

Materials: Sport weight yarn, 2 oz lt purple; ⅓ oz purple; ¼ oz raspberry; 1 oz cranberry
Size D aluminum crochet hook, or size required for gauge
Size F aluminum crochet hook (for edging)

Gauge: With size D hook, one square = 4½″ × 4½″
With size D hook, 10 sts and 6 rows = 2″

INSTRUCTIONS

Square (make 4 with purple as color A and 2 with raspberry as color A)

With size D hook and color A, ch 4; join to form a ring.

Rnd 1: Ch 3 (counts as a dc), 15 dc in ring; join in 3rd ch of beg ch-3: 16 dc. Do not turn; work in rnds.

Rnd 2: Sl st between beg ch-3 of prev rnd and next dc, ch 5 (counts as a dc and ch 2); (dc in between next 2 dc, ch 2) 15 times; join in 3rd ch of beg ch-5: 16 ch-2 sps.

Rnd 3: Sl st in next ch-2 sp, ch 3 (counts as a dc), 2 dc in same sp; (ch 1, sk next dc, 3 dc in next ch-2 sp) 15 times; ch 1, sk next dc; join in 3rd ch of beg ch-3; finish off.

Rnd 4: Join pink in any ch-1 sp; sc in same sp; * (ch 3, sk next 3 dc, sc in next ch-1 sp) 3 times; ch 5: corner lp made; sc in next ch-1 sp; rep from * 3 times more, ending last rep without working last sc; join in first sc.

Rnd 5: Sl st in next ch-3 sp, ch 3 (counts as a dc in this and following rnd), 2 dc in same sp; * (ch 1, sk next sc, 3 dc in next ch-3 sp) twice, ch 1; in next ch-5 corner lp work (5 dc, ch 2, 5 dc): corner made; rep from * 3 times more; ch 1, sk next sc; join in 3rd ch of beg ch-3; finish off.

Rnd 6: Join cranberry in any ch-2 corner sp; ch 3 (counts as a dc), in same sp work (trc, dc): corner made; * (dc between next 2 dc) 4 times; † dc in next ch-1 sp, (dc in between next 2 dc) twice †; rep from † to † twice more; dc in next ch-1 sp, (dc in sp between next 2 dc) 4 times; in next corner ch-2 sp work (dc, trc, dc): corner made; rep from * 3 times more,

ending last rep without working last (dc, trc, dc); join in 3rd ch of beg ch-3; finish off.

Joining

Join squares in 2 rows of 3 squares, referring to photo for placemat. To join squares, hold two squares with right sides tog. Carefully matching sts on both squares and with cranberry, sew with overcast sts in inner lps (see page 10) only across side, beg and ending with one corner st. Join in rows; then sew rows tog in same manner, being sure that all four-corner junctions are firmly joined.

Center section

Hold one strip of 3 squares with right side facing you and with long edge at top. Join cranberry in first dc in upper right-hand corner.

Row 1 (right side): Ch 3 (counts as a dc in this and all following rows), * dc in next 20 dc, dc in next seam, rep from * once more; dc in next 21 dc; 64 dc; finish off.

Row 2: With right side facing you, join pink in 3rd ch of beg ch-3 of prev row; ch 3, dc in next 63 dc; ch 3, turn.

Row 3: Dc in each dc, dc in turning ch; ch 3, turn. Rep Rnd 3 until placemat measures 12″. Finish off.

Last Row: With right side facing you, join cranberry in first dc, ch 3, dc in next 62 dc, dc in turning ch; finish off.

Finishing

Hold placemat and second strip of squares with right sides tog. Sew in same manner as squares were joined.

Edging

Hold placemat with right side facing you and long side at top. With size F hook, join cranberry in first dc in upper right-hand corner; * sk next 2 dc, 5 dc in next dc, sk next 2 dc, sl st in next dc; rep from * around placemat (counting end st of each row of center section as a dc), adjusting sts slightly so that last sl st is made in joining sl st. Finish off and weave in all ends.

❦ Colorful Towels ❦

Size: 16″ × 30″

Materials: Sport weight, 3-ply cotton yarn (11 oz total for one towel) in following colors:

Towel A: 1½ oz dark pink, 1½ oz purple, 1 oz lavender, 1¼ oz pink, and 6 oz red

Towel B: 2 oz green, 2 oz dark blue, 1 oz turquoise, and 6 oz medium blue

Towel C: 1¼ oz yellow, ¾ oz dark pink, 1¾ oz lavendar, ½ oz purple, ¾ oz dark red, and 6 oz red

Size O steel crochet hook

Gauge: 11 dc = 2″; 5 rows = 2″

INSTRUCTIONS

Referring to Color Chart for each rnd for Towel A, B, or C, ch 75 with color specified for Rnd 1.

Rnd 1: Dc in 3rd ch from hook, in same ch, work 2 dc: first dc-group made; * ch 1, sk next 2 chs, 3 dc in next ch: dc-group made; rep from * 22 times more; ch 1, sk next 2 chs, in last ch, work (dc-group, ch 1 [corner sp]) 3 times; working in opposite side of ch, † sk next 2 chs, work dc-group in next ch, ch 1 †; rep from † to † 22 times more; sk next 2 chs, in beg ch, work (dc-group, ch 1 [corner sp]) twice; join in 3rd ch of beg ch-3: 52 dc-groups and ch-1 sps; finish off color.

Rnd 2: Join new color in ch-1 sp following last corner sp made in prev rnd; ch 3 (counts as first dc), in same sp, work 2 dc: beg dc-group made; * † ch 1, sk next dc-group, in next ch-1 sp, work dc-group †; rep from * 22 times more; ch 1, sk next dc-group, in next ch-1 corner sp, work (dc-group, ch 1 [corner sp], dc-group): double dc-group made; ch 1, sk next dc-group, in next ch-1 corner sp, work double dc-group; rep from

Color Chart

Rnd	Towel A	Towel B	Towel C
1	Dark Pink	Green	Yellow
2	Purple	Dark Blue	Dark Pink
3	Dark Pink	Green	Yellow
4-6	Dark Red	Medium Blue	Red
7	Lavender	Dark Blue	Lavender
8	Purple	Green	Purple
9	Lavender	Dark Blue	Lavender
10-12	Dark Red	Medium Blue	Red
13	Dark Pink	Green	Yellow
14	Purple	Turquoise	Dark Pink
15	Dark Pink	Green	Yellow
16-18	Dark Red	Medium Blue	Red
19	Pink	Dark Blue	Lavender
20	Purple	Turquoise	Dark Red
21	Pink	Dark Blue	Lavender
22-26	Dark Red	Medium Blue	Red

† to † 24 times more; (ch 1, sk next dc-group, in next ch-1 corner sp, work double dc-group) twice; ch 1, join in 3rd ch of beg ch-3: 56 dc-groups and ch-1 sps; finish off color.

Rnd 3: Join new color in ch-1 sp to left of last double dc-group worked in prev rnd; in same ch-1 sp, work beg dc-group; * † ch 1, sk next dc-group, in next ch-1 sp, work dc-group †; rep from * 23 times more; †† ch 1, in next ch-1 corner sp, work double dc-group; ch 1, sk next dc-group, in next ch-1 sp, work dc-group, ch 1, sk next dc-group, in next ch-1 corner sp, work double dc-group ††; rep from † to † 25 times more; rep from †† to †† once; ch 1, join in 3rd ch of beg ch-3: 60 dc-groups and ch-1 sps.

Rnd 4: Join new color in ch-1 sp to left of last double dc-group worked in prev rnd; in same ch-1 sp, work beg dc-group; * † ch 1, sk next dc-group, in next ch-1 sp, work dc-group †; rep from * 24 times more; †† ch 1, in next ch-1 corner sp, work double dc-group, (ch 1, sk next dc-group, in next ch-1 sp, work dc-group, ch 1) twice; sk next dc-group, in next ch-1 corner sp, work double dc-group ††; rep from † to † 26 times more; rep from †† to †† once; ch 1, join in 3rd ch of beg ch-3: 64 dc-groups and ch-1 sps; sl st in next 3 dc of next dc-group, sl st in next ch-1 sp.

Rnd 5: In same ch-1 sp, work beg dc-group; * † ch 1, sk next dc-group, in next ch-1 sp, work dc-group †; rep from * 24 times more; †† ch 1, in next ch-1 corner sp, work double dc-group, (ch 1, sk next dc-group, in next ch-1 sp, work dc-group, ch 1) 3 times; sk next dc-group, in next ch-1 corner sp, work double dc-group ††; rep from † to † 27 times more; rep from †† to †† once; ch 1, sk next dc-group, in next ch-1 sp, work dc-group; ch 1, join in 3rd ch of beg ch-3: 68 dc-groups and ch-1 sps; sl st in next 3 dc of next dc-group, sl st in next ch-1 sp.

Rnd 6: In same ch-1 sp, work beg dc-group; * † ch 1, sk next dc-group, in next ch-1 sp, work dc-group †; rep from * 24

times more; †† ch 1, in next ch-1 corner sp, work double dc-group, (ch 1, sk next dc-group, in next ch-1 sp, work dc-group, ch 1) 4 times; sk next dc-group, in next ch-1 corner sp, work double dc-group ††; rep from † to † 28 times more; rep from †† to †† once; (ch 1, sk next dc-group, in next ch-1 sp, work dc-group) twice, ch 1; join in 3rd ch of beg ch-3: 72 dc-groups and ch-1 sps; finish off color.

Rnd 7: Join new color in ch-1 sp to left of last double dc-group worked in prev rnd; in same ch-1 sp, work beg dc-group; * † ch 1, sk next dc-group, in next ch-1 sp, work dc-group †; rep from * 27 times more; †† ch 1, in next ch-1 corner sp, work double dc-group, (ch 1, sk next dc-group, in next ch-1 sp, work dc-group, ch 1) 5 times; sk next dc-group, in next ch-1 corner sp, work double dc-group ††; rep from † to † 29 times more; rep from †† to †† once; ch 1, join in 3rd ch of beg ch-3: 76 dc-groups and ch-1 sps; finish off color.

Rnd 8: Join new color in ch-1 sp to left of last double dc-group worked in prev rnd; in same ch-1 sp, work beg dc-group; * † ch 1, sk next dc-group, in next ch-1 sp, work dc-group †; rep from * 28 times more; †† ch 1, in next ch-1 corner sp, work double dc-group, (ch 1, sk next dc-group, in next ch-1 sp, work dc-group, ch 1) 6 times; sk next dc-group, in next ch-1 corner sp, work double dc-group ††, rep from † to † 30 times more; rep from †† to †† once; ch 1, join in 3rd ch of beg ch-3: 80 dc-groups and ch-1 sps; finish off color.

Rnd 9: Join new color in ch-1 sp to left of last double dc-group worked in prev rnd; in same ch-1 sp, work beg dc-group; * † ch 1, sk next dc-group, in next ch-1 sp, work dc-group †; rep from * 29 times more; †† ch 1, in next ch-1 corner sp, work double dc group, (ch 1, sk next dc-group, in next ch-1 sp, work dc-group, ch 1) 7 times; sk next dc-group, in next ch-1 corner sp, work double dc-group ††; rep from † to † 31 times more; rep from †† to †† once; ch 1, join in 3rd ch of beg ch-3: 84 dc-groups and ch-1 sps; finish off color.

Rnd 10: Join new color in ch-1 sp to left of last double dc-group worked in prev rnd; in same ch-1 sp, work beg dc-group; * † ch 1, sk next dc-group, in next ch-1 sp, work dc-group †; rep from * 30 times more; †† ch 1, in next ch-1 corner sp, work double dc-group, (ch 1, sk next dc-group, in next ch-1 sp, work dc-group, ch 1) 8 times; sk next dc-group, in next ch-1 corner sp, work double dc-group ††; rep from † to † 32 times; rep from †† to †† once; ch 1, join in 3rd ch of beg ch-3: 88 dc-groups and ch-1 sps; sl st in next 3 dc of next dc-group, sl st in next ch-1 sp.

Rnd 11: In same ch-1 sp, work beg dc-group; * † ch 1, sk next dc-group, in next ch-1 sp, work dc-group †; rep from * 30 times more; †† ch 1, in next ch-1 corner sp, work double dc-group, (ch 1, sk next dc-group, in next ch-1 sp, work dc-group, ch 1) 9 times; sk next dc-group, in next ch-1 corner sp, work double dc-group ††; rep from † to † 33 times; rep from †† to †† once; ch 1, sk next dc-group, in next ch-1 sp, work dc-group; ch 1, join in 3rd ch of beg ch-3: 92 dc-groups and ch-1 sps; sl st in next 3 dc of next dc-group, sl st in next ch-1 sp.

Rnd 12: In same ch-1 sp, work beg dc-group; * † ch 1, sk next dc-group, in next ch-1 sp, work dc-group †; rep from * 30 times more; †† ch 1, in next ch-1 corner sp, work double dc-group, (ch 1, sk next dc-group, in next ch-1 sp, work dc-group, ch 1) 10 times; sk next dc-group, in next ch-1 corner sp, work double dc-group ††; rep from † to † 34 times; rep from †† to †† once; (ch 1, sk next dc-group, in next ch-1 sp, work dc-group, ch 1) twice; join in 3rd ch of beg ch-3: 96 dc-groups and ch-1 sps; finish off color.

Rnd 13: Join new color in ch-1 sp to left of last double dc-group worked in prev rnd; in same ch-1 sp, work beg dc-group; * † ch 1, sk next dc-group, in next ch-1 sp, work dc-group †; rep from * 33 times more; †† ch 1, in next ch-1 corner sp, work double dc-group, (ch 1, sk next dc-group, in next ch-1 sp, work dc-group, ch 1) 11 times; sk next dc-group, in next ch-1 corner sp, work double dc-group ††; rep from † to † 35 times more; rep from †† to †† once; ch 1, join in 3rd ch of beg ch-3: 100 dc-groups and ch-1 sps; finish off color.

Rnd 14: Join new color in ch-1 sp to left of last double dc-group worked in prev rnd; in same ch-1 sp, work beg dc-group; * † ch 1, sk next dc-group, in next ch-1 sp, work dc-group †; rep from * 34 times more; †† ch 1, in next ch-1 corner sp, work double dc-group, (ch 1, sk next dc-group, in next ch-1 sp, work dc-group, ch 1) 12 times; sk next dc-group, in next ch-1 corner sp, work double dc-group ††; rep from † to † 36 times more; rep from †† to †† once; ch 1, join in 3rd ch of beg ch-3: 104 dc-groups and ch-1 sps; finish off color.

Rnd 15: Join new color in ch-1 sp to left of last double dc-group worked in prev rnd; in same ch-1 sp, work beg dc-group; * † ch 1, sk next dc-group, in next ch-1 sp, work dc-group †; rep from * 35 times more; †† ch 1, in next ch-1 corner sp, work double dc-group, (ch 1, sk next dc-group, in next ch-1 sp, work dc-group, ch 1) 13 times; sk next dc-group, in next ch-1 corner sp, work double dc-group ††; rep from † to † 36 times more; rep from †† to †† once; ch 1, join in 3rd ch of beg ch-3: 108 dc-groups and ch-1 sps; finish off color.

Rnd 16: Join new color in ch-1 sp to left of last double dc-group worked in prev rnd; in same ch-1 sp, work beg dc-group; * † ch 1, sk next dc-group, in next ch-1 sp, work dc-group †; rep from * 36 times more; †† ch 1, in next ch-1 corner sp, work double dc-group, (ch 1, sk next dc-group, in next ch-1 sp, work dc-group, ch 1) 14 times; sk next dc-group, in next ch-1 corner sp, work double dc-group ††; rep from † to † 38 times more; rep from †† to †† once; ch 1, join in 3rd ch of beg ch-3: 112 dc-groups and ch-1 sps; sl st in next 3 dc of next dc-group, sl st in next ch-1 sp.

Rnd 17: In same ch-1 sp, work beg dc-group; * † ch 1, sk next dc-group, in next ch-1 sp, work dc-group †; rep from * 36 times more; †† ch 1, in next ch-1 corner sp, work double dc-group, (ch 1, sk next dc-group, in next ch-1 sp, work dc-group, ch 1) 15 times; sk next dc-group, in next ch-1 corner sp, work double dc-group ††; rep from † to † 39 times more; rep from †† to †† once; ch 1, sk next dc-group, in next ch-1 sp, work dc-group; ch 1, join in 3rd ch of beg ch-3: 116 dc-groups and ch-1 sps; sl st in next 3 dc of next dc-group, sl st in next ch-1 sp.

Rnd 18: In same ch-1 sp, work beg dc-group; * † ch 1, sk next dc-group, in next ch-1 sp, work dc-group †; rep from * 37 times more; †† ch 1, in next ch-1 corner sp, work double dc-group, (ch 1, sk next dc-group, in next ch-1 sp, work dc-group, ch 1) 16 times; sk next dc-group, in next ch-1 corner sp, work double dc-group ††; rep from † to † 40 times more; rep from †† to †† once; (ch 1, sk next dc-group, in next ch-1 sp, work dc-group, ch 1) twice; join in 3rd ch of beg ch-3: 120 dc-groups and ch-1 sps; finish off color.

Rnd 19: Join new color in ch-1 sp to left of last double dc-group worked in prev rnd; in same ch-1 sp, work beg dc-group; * † ch 1, sk next dc-group, in next ch-1 sp, work dc-group †; rep from * 39 times more; †† ch 1, in next ch-1 corner sp, work double dc-group, (ch 1, sk next dc-group, in next ch-1 sp, work dc-group, ch 1) 17 times; sk next dc-group, in next ch-1 corner sp, work double dc-group ††; rep from † to † 41 times more; rep from †† to †† once; ch 1, join in 3rd ch of beg ch-3: 124 dc-groups and ch-1 sps; finish off color.

Rnd 20: Join new color in ch-1 sp to left of last double dc-group worked in prev rnd; in same ch-1 sp, work beg dc-group; * † ch 1, sk next dc-group, in next ch-1 sp, work dc-group †; rep from * 40 times more; †† ch 1, in next ch-1 corner sp, work double dc-group, (ch 1, sk next dc-group, in next ch-1 sp, work dc-group, ch 1) 18 times; sk next dc-group, in next ch-1 corner sp, work double dc-group ††; rep from † to † 42 times more; rep from †† to †† once; ch 1, join in 3rd ch of beg ch-3: 128 dc-groups and ch-1 sps; finish off color.

Rnd 21: Join new color in ch-1 sp to left of last double dc-group worked in prev rnd; in same ch-1 sp, work beg dc-group; * † ch 1, sk next dc-group, in next ch-1 sp, work dc-group †; rep from * 41 times more; †† ch 1, in next ch-1 corner sp, work double dc-group, (ch-1, sk next dc-group, in next ch-1 sp, work dc-group, ch 1) 19 times; sk next dc-group, in next ch-1 corner sp, work double dc-group ††; rep from † to † 43 times more; rep from †† to †† once; ch 1, join in 3rd ch of beg ch-3: 132 dc-groups and ch-1 sps; finish off color.

Rnd 22: Join new color in ch-1 sp to left of last double dc-group worked in prev rnd; in same ch-1 sp, work beg dc-group; * † ch 1, sk next dc group, in next ch-1 sp, work dc-group †; rep from * 42 times more; †† ch 1, in next ch-1 corner sp, work double dc-group, (ch 1, sk next dc-group, in next ch-1 sp, work dc-group, ch 1) 20 times; sk next dc-group, in next ch-1 corner sp, work double dc-group ††; rep from † to † 44 times more; rep from †† to †† once; ch 1, join in 3rd ch of beg ch-3: 136 dc-groups and ch-1 sps; sl st in next 3 dc of next dc-group, sl st in next ch-1 sp.

Rnd 23: In same ch-1 sp, work beg dc-group; * † ch 1, sk next dc-group, in next ch-1 sp, work dc-group †; rep from * 41 times more; †† ch 1, in next ch-1 corner sp, work double dc-group, (ch 1, sk next dc-group, in next ch-1 sp, work dc-group, ch 1) 21 times; sk next dc-group, in next ch-1 corner sp, work double dc-group ††; rep from † to † 45 times more; rep from †† to †† once: ch 1, sk next dc-group, in next ch-1 sp, work dc-group; ch 1, join in 3rd ch of beg ch-3: 140 dc-groups and ch-1 sps; sl st in next 3 dc of next dc-group, sl st in next ch-1 sp.

Rnd 24: In same ch-1 sp, work beg dc-group; * † ch 1, sk next dc-group, in next ch-1 sp, work dc-group †; rep from * 42 times more; †† ch 1, in next ch-1 corner sp, work double dc-group, (ch 1, sk next dc-group, in next ch-1 sp, work dc-group, ch 1) 22 times; sk next dc-group, in next ch-1 corner sp, work double dc-group ††; rep from † to † 46 times more; rep from †† to †† once; (ch 1, sk next dc-group, in next ch-1 sp, work dc-group) twice; ch 1, join in 3rd ch of beg ch-3: 144 dc-groups and ch-1 sps; ch 1.

Rnd 25: † Sc in next 3 dc, sc in next ch-1 sp †; rep from † to † 43 times more; †† sc in next 3 dc, 3 sc in next ch-1 corner sp, sc in next 3 dc ††; rep from † to † 22 times more; rep from †† to †† once; rep from † to † 46 times more; rep from †† to †† once; rep from † to † 22 times more; rep from †† to †† once; rep from † to † twice; join in first sc: 580 sc.

Rnd 26: Sc in each sc: 580 sc; finish off and weave in ends.

Hanging Loop

With same color as Rnd 26, ch 31.

Row 1: Sc in 2nd ch from hook, sc in each ch: 30 sc; ch 1, turn.

Row 2: Sc in each sc: 30 sc; finish off and weave in ends.

Fold hanging Loop in half and sew both ends, using overcast st, on wrong side of Rnd 25 in center of one short end of towel.

Pink Potholders

Size: 7⅜" diameter

Materials: Worsted weight yarn in following colors, ½ oz pink, ½ oz beige, ¼ oz dark rose, and ¼ oz white
Size F aluminum crochet hook

Gauge: 4 sc = 1"; 4 rows = 1"

INSTRUCTIONS

Note: Long sc is worked in base of next st of prev rnd. Insert hook in same place as st of prev rnd, keeping sts loose.

With pink, ch 5, join with sl st to form a ring.

Rnd 1: Ch 2 (counts as hdc), work 9 hdc in ring: 10 hdc.

Rnd 2: 2 hdc in each hdc: 20 hdc; finish off pink.

Rnd 3: Join white in last hdc worked; hdc in each hdc: 20 hdc.

Rnd 4: * 2 hdc in next hdc, hdc in next hdc; rep from * 9 times more: 30 hdc; finish off white.

Rnd 5: Join dark rose in last hdc worked; * sc in next 2 hdc, sc at base of next hdc of prev row: long sc made; in same hdc, work long sc; rep from * 9 times more: 40 sc; finish off dark rose.

Rnd 6: Join white in last sc worked; sc in each sc: 40 sc.

Rnd 7: * 2 hdc in next sc, hdc in next 3 sc; rep from * 8 times more; 2 hdc in next sc, hdc in next 2 sc, 2 hdc in next sc: 51 hdc; finish off white.

Rnd 8: Join pink in last hdc worked; * 2 long sc in base of next hdc of prev row, sc in next 2 hdc; rep from * 16 times more: 68 sc; finish off pink.

Rnd 9: Join beige in last sc worked; sc in each sc: 68 sc.

Rnd 10: Hdc in each sc: 68 hdc; finish off beige.

Rnd 11: Join dark rose in last hdc worked; * sc in next 3 hdc, 2 long sc in base of next hdc of prev row; rep from * 16 times more: 84 sc; finish off dark rose.

Rnd 12: Join beige in last hdc worked; sc in each sc: 84 sc.

Rnd 13: Hdc in each sc: 84 hdc; finish off beige.

Rnd 14: Join pink in last hdc worked; ch 12, sl st in first ch to form a hanging lp; * sc in next 2 hdc, 2 long sc in base of next hdc of prev row; rep from * 27 times more: 108 sc; work 20 sc in hanging lp; join with sl st in first sc, finish off and weave in ends.

Chrysanthemum Table Runner

Size: About 13″ × 24″

Materials: Sport weight yarn, 3 oz green; ¼ oz pale yellow; scraps of various contrasting floral colors
Size E aluminum crochet hook, or size required for gauge

Gauge: one square = 3¾″ × 3¾″
  11 sc = 2″
  11 sc rows = 2″

INSTRUCTIONS

Motif (make 18)

With pale yellow, ch 4, join to form a ring.

Rnd 1: Ch 3 (counts as a dc), 11 dc in ring; join in 3rd ch of beg ch-3: 12 dc; finish off pale yellow.

Rnd 2: Join a contrasting floral color in last dc worked; ch 5 (counts as a dc and ch 2), * dc in next dc, ch 2; rep from * 10 times more; join in 3rd ch of beg ch-5: 12 ch-2 sps.

Rnd 3: Sl st in next ch-2 sp, ch 1, 3 sc in same sp; * sk next dc, 3 sc in next ch-2 sp; rep from * 10 times more; join in first sc: 36 sc.

Rnd 4: Ch 1, * sc in next 2 sc, 2 sc in next sc; rep from * 11 times more; join in first sc: 48 sc.

Rnd 5: Ch 1, * in next sc work (sc, dc), ch 1; in next sc work (dc, sc), sk next 2 sc; rep from * 11 times more: 12 shells made; finish off and weave in ends.

Rnd 6: Join green in ch-1 sp of any shell; ch 1, sc in same sp; * ch 5, sc in ch-1 sp of next shell; rep from * 10 times more; ch 5; join in first sc: 12 ch-5 sps.

Rnd 7: Sl st in next ch-5 sp, 5 sc in same sp; * sk next sc, 5 sc in next ch-5 sp; rep from * 10 times more; sk next sc; join in first sc: 60 sc.

Rnd 8: Ch 1, * sc in next 8 sc, hdc in next 3 sc, 3 dc in next sc, hdc in next 3 sc; rep from * 3 times more; join in first sc; finish off and weave in ends.

Joining

Join motifs in 6 rows of 3 motifs. To join, hold two motifs with right sides tog. Carefully matching sts and with green, sew with overcast st in inner lps (see page 10) only across side, beg and ending in center dc of 3-dc corner group and being sure all four-corner junctions are firmly joined.

Edging

Hold table runner with right side facing you and long edge at top; join green in center dc of upper right-hand corner.

Rnd 1: Ch 1, 3 sc in same dc as joining; * sc in each st around table runner, working 3 sc in each center dc of each rem outer corner; join in first sc.

Rnd 2: Ch 1, * sc in next 2 sc, ch 3, sl st in 3rd ch from hook: picot made; rep from * around; join in first sc; finish off and weave in ends.

124

Chapter 6
GRANNY'S GIFTS

These projects make wonderful gifts—accessories ranging from a bright shawl to slippers, bags and hats to a coat for Man's (and Woman's!) best friend. We won't tell if you want to keep them for yourself!

Shoulder Bag and Hat

Size:

Shoulder Bag = 9″ square
Finished Hat = 22″ around

Materials: Worsted weight yarn; 2½ oz cream, 3½ oz light brown, 3½ oz medium brown, 3 oz dark brown
Size D and E aluminum crochet hook, or size required for gauge

Gauge: 5 dc = 1″; 5 rows = 2″

INSTRUCTIONS

SHOULDER BAG

With Size E hook and referring to colors for each rnd for Rnds 1 through 10 below, work 10-rnd Traditional Granny Square on page 11.

Rnd 1: Cream

Rnd 2: Lt brown

Rnd 3: Med brown

Rnd 4: Dk brown

Rnd 5: Med brown

Rnd 6: Lt brown

Rnd 7: Cream

Rnd 8: Lt brown

Rnd 9: Med brown

Rnd 10: Dk brown

Rep Rnds 1 through 10 for opposite side of shoulder bag.

Joining

With size D hook and with wrong sides together, join dark brown in top left-hand corner of both squares in ch-2 corner sp, ch 1.

Row 1: In same ch-2 corner sp, work 2 sc; carefully matching sts and sps, * † (sc in next 3 dc, sc in next ch-1 sp) † 9 times, sc in next 3 dc, in next ch-2 corner sp, work 3 sc; rep from * once more; rep from † to † 9 times, sc in next 3 dc, in next ch-2 sp, work 2 sc; finish off and weave in ends.

Shoulder Bag Opening Edging

Hold bag with right side facing you and opening at top; join dark brown in sc at either side seam.

Rnd 1: Ch 3 (counts as first dc), work 2 dc in same sc, ch 3; † sk next 3 dc, in next ch-1 sp, work 3 dc, ch 3 †; rep from † to † 8 times more; in sc at side seam, work 3 dc, ch 3; rep from † to † 9 times; join in 3rd ch of beg ch-3; finish off and weave in ends.

Fringe

Following Fringe instructions on page 9, make single knot fringe. Cut 8″ strands of med brown; use 8 strands for each knot. Tie knots in each sp along sides and bottom of bag.

Shoulder Bag Closing Twisted Cord

Step 1: Cut 8 strands of dark brown yarn, each 4 times the closing cord length (26″).

Step 2: Make a lp at each end of strands, sufficient in size to slip over a door knob or onto a hook.

Step 3: Place one lp on knob or hook.

Step 4: Slip other lp at opposite end of index finger (or several fingers depending on size of lp) or onto a pencil. (Note: For a quicker method, tie this looped end to one beater of an electric mixer.)

Step 5: Holding strands taut, twist strands in one direction until firm and slightly kinky along the entire length. (Note: For quicker method, twist strands with an electric mixer—remember it is better to over beat than under beat.)

Step 6: Keeping strands taut, fold twisted strands over in half, then slip lp off finger(s) or pencil (or beater) and place onto knob or hook with other looped end.

Step 7: Still keeping strands taut, let strands twist together using the thumb and finger of one hand to guide and smooth strands as they form into a twisted cord.

Step 8: Knot each end of cord, and cut off excess cording. Trim yarn ends evenly at each end of cord.

Weave cord through sps of Rnd 1 of Shoulder Bag Opening Edging.

Shoulder Bag Carrying Strap

Step 1: Cut 12 strands of dark brown yarn, each 4 times the Shoulder Bag Strap length (40").

Rep Steps 2 through 8 of Shoulder Bag Closing Twisted Cord instructions.

Sew each end of Carrying Strap to inside of Shoulder Bag at side seams below Row 1 of Shoulder Bag Opening Edging, stitching securely.

HAT

With cream and Size E hook, ch 6; join to form a ring.

Rnd 1: Ch 3 (counts as first dc in this and following rnds), 2 dc in ring, ch 1; (3 dc in ring, ch 1) 3 times; join in 3rd ch of beg ch-3: 4, 3-dc groups and 4 ch-1 sps; finish off cream.

Rnd 2: Join light brown in any ch-1 sp; in same ch-1 sp, ch 3, in same sp work (2 dc, ch 1, 3 dc), ch 1; * sk next 3 dc, in next ch-1 sp, work (3 dc, ch 1, 3 dc), ch 1; rep from * twice; join in 3rd ch of beg ch-3: 8, 3-dc groups and 8 ch-1 sps; finish off light brown.

Rnd 3: Join medium brown in any ch-1 corner sp; ch 3, in same sp, work (2 dc, ch 1, 3 dc), ch 1; * † sk next 3 dc, in next ch-1 sp, work 3 dc, ch 1 †, sk next 3 dc, in next ch-1 corner sp, work (3 dc, ch 1, 3 dc), ch 1; rep from * twice; rep from † to † once; join in 3rd ch of beg ch-3: 12, 3-dc groups and 12 ch-1 sps; finish off medium brown.

Rnd 4: Join dark brown in any ch-1 corner sp, ch 3, in same ch-1 sp, work (2 dc, ch 1, 3 dc), ch 1; * † (sk next 3 dc, in next ch-1 sp, work 3 dc, ch 1) † twice; sk next 3 dc, in next ch-1 corner sp, work (3 dc, ch 1, 3 dc), ch 1; rep from * twice; rep from † to † once; join in 3rd ch of beg ch-3: 16, 3-dc groups and 16 ch-1 sps; finish off dark brown.

Rnd 5: Join medium brown in any ch-1 corner sp, ch 3, in same ch-1 sp, work (2 dc, ch 1, 3 dc), ch 1; * † (sk next 3 dc, in next ch-1 sp, work 3 dc, ch 1) † 3 times; sk next 3 dc, in next ch-1 corner sp, work (3 dc, ch 1, 3 dc), ch 1; rep from * twice; rep from † to † once; join in 3rd ch of beg ch-3: 20, 3-dc groups and 20 ch-1 sps; finish off medium brown.

Rnd 6: Join light brown in any ch-1 corner sp, ch 3, in same ch-1 sp, work (2 dc, ch 1, 3 dc), ch 1; * † (sk next 3 dc, in next ch-1 sp, work 3 dc, ch 1) † 4 times; sk next 3 dc, in next ch-1 corner sp, work (3 dc, ch 1, 3 dc), ch 1; rep from * twice; rep from † to † once; join in 3rd ch of beg ch-3: 24, 3-dc groups and 24 ch-1 sps; finish off light brown.

Rnd 7: Join cream in any ch-1 corner sp, ch 3, in same sp, work 2 dc, ch 1; * † (sk next 3 dc, in next ch-1 sp, work 3 dc, ch 1) † 5 times; sk next 3 dc, in next ch-1 corner sp, work 3 dc, ch 1; rep from * twice; rep from † to † once; join in 3rd ch of beg ch-3: 24, 3-dc groups and 24 ch-1 sps; finish off cream.

Rnd 8: Join light brown in any ch-1 sp; ch 3, in same ch-1 sp, work 2 dc, ch 1; * sk next 3 dc, in next ch-1 sp, work 3 dc, ch 1; rep from * 22 times more; join in 3rd ch of beg ch-3: 24, 3-dc groups and 24 ch-1 sps; finish off color.

Referring to colors for each rnd for Rnds 9 through 13 below, rep Rnd 8.

Rnd 9: Medium Brown.

Rnd 10: Dark Brown.

Rnd 11: Medium Brown.

Rnd 12: Light Brown.

Rnd 13: Cream.

Rnd 14: Join light brown in any ch-1 sp; ch 3 (counts as first dc); * dc in next 3 dc, dc in next ch-1 sp; rep from * 22 times more; dc in next 3 dc; join in 3rd ch of beg ch-3: 96 dc; finish off light brown.

Rnd 15: Join medium brown in any dc, ch 3 (counts as first dc); dc in each dc; join in 3rd ch of beg ch-3: 96 dc; finish off medium brown.

Rnd 16: Join light brown in any dc; rep Rnd 15; finish off light brown.

Rnd 17: On wrong side, join cream between any 2 dc, ch 5 (counts as first dc and ch 2); * sk next 3 dc, dc under lps and between next dc, ch 2; rep from * 30 times more; sk next 3 dc, join in 3rd ch of beg ch-5; 32 ch-2 sps; finish off cream.

Rnd 18: Join light brown in any ch-2 sp; ch 3 (counts as first dc), in same ch-2 sp, work 2 dc, ch 2; * sk next dc, in next ch-2 sp, work 3 dc, ch 2; rep from * 30 times more; join in 3rd ch of beg ch-3: 32, 3-dc groups and 32 ch-2 sps; finish off light brown.

Rnd 19: Join medium brown in any ch-2 sp; ch 3 (counts as first dc), in same ch-2 sp, work 2 dc, ch 2; * sk next 3 dc, in next ch-2 sp, work 3 dc, ch 2; rep from * 30 times more; join in 3rd ch of beg ch-3: 32, 3-dc groups and 32 ch-2 sps; finish off medium brown.

Rnd 20: Join dark brown in any ch-2 sp; rep Rnd 19; finish off dark brown.

Rnd 21: Join medium brown in any ch-2 sp; rep Rnd 19; finish off medium brown.

Rnd 22: With Size D hook, join light brown in any ch-2 sp; ch 1, sc in same ch-2 sp; * sc in next 3 dc, sc in next ch-2 sp; rep from * 30 times more; join in first sc: 128 sc; do not finish off.

Rnd 23: Ch 1; working from left to right, work rev sc (see page 9) in same joining sc; work rev sc in each sc; join in first rev sc; finish off and weave in ends.

Shopping Bag

Size: About 14″ × 14″

Materials: Worsted weight yarn, 2 oz cream; 5 oz colors of your choice

Size G aluminum crochet hook, or size required for gauge

Wooden purse handle (available in craft or hobby stores)

Gauge: 3-rnd square = 3½″

INSTRUCTIONS

Following instructions for Traditional Granny Square #1 on page 11, make thirty-two 3-rnd squares. Make 16 squares using colors of your choice for 3 rnds and 16 squares using colors of your choice for 2 rnds and cream for 3rd rnd.

Joining

For front and back pieces, join 16 squares in 4 rows of 4 squares, referring to photo for placement of squares. To join squares, hold two squares with right sides tog. Carefully matching sts on both squares and with cream, sew with overcast st in inner lps (see page 10) only across side, beg and ending with one corner st. Join squares in rows; then sew rows tog in same manner, being sure that all four-corner junctions are firmly joined.

Assembling

With right sides of front and back sections tog, carefully match sts. Sew tog on sides and bottom, leaving top open.

Handle casings

With front of bag facing you, join cream in ch-2 sp in upper right-hand corner.

Row 1: Ch 3 (counts as a dc), * (dc in next 3 dc, dc in ch-1 sp) twice, dc in next 3 dc, dc in next ch-2 sp, dc in joining, dc in next ch-2 sp; rep from * 3 times more; ch 3, turn.

Row 2: Dc in each dc, dc in top of turning ch; finish off.

With back of bag facing you, rep casing instructions.

Finishing

Fold casings to inside of bag and insert handles; sew casings securely in place.

Fringe

Following Fringe instructions on page 9, make single knot fringe. Cut 8″ strands of colors of your choice; use 3 strands of same color for each knot. Tie knots evenly spaced (about every 3 sts) across bottom edge of bag. Trim ends evenly.

Circle-In-A-Square Shawl

Size: 60″ on longest side

Materials: Sport weight yarn, 8 oz black; 12 oz colors of your choice
Size D aluminum crochet hook, or size required for gauge

Gauge: Square = 4½″

INSTRUCTIONS

Following instructions for Wagon Wheel Square #2 on page 13, make 55 squares with colors of your choice for Rnds 1 through 5 and with black for Rnd 6.

Wagon Wheel Half Square *(make 11)*

With first color, ch 8, join to form a ring.

Rnd 1: Ch 3 (counts as a dc), 10 dc in ring; 11 dc; finish off. Do not turn; work in half rnds.

Rnd 2: Join same color between first 2 dc of prev rnd; ch 5 (counts as a dc and ch-2 sp); (dc between next 2 dc, ch 2) 8 times; dc between last 2 dc: 9 ch-2 sps; finish off.

Rnd 3: Join same color in first ch-2 sp of prev rnd; ch 3 (counts as a dc), 2 dc in same sp; (ch 1, 3 dc in next sp) 8 times: 9, 3-dc groups; finish off.

Rnd 4: Join new color in 3rd ch of beg ch-3 of prev rnd; ch 5: half corner made; (sk next 3-dc group, sc in next ch-1 sp, ch 3) 3 times; ch 5, sc in next ch-1 sp: corner made; (ch 3, sc between next pair of 3-dc groups) 3 times; ch 5, sl st in top of last dc of prev rnd: half corner made; finish off.

Rnd 5: Join same color in first ch-5 half-corner sp of last rnd; ch 3 (counts as a dc), 4 dc in same sp: half corner made; (3 dc in next ch-3 sp) twice; in next ch-5 corner sp work (5 dc, ch 2, 5 dc): corner made; (3 dc in next ch-3 sp) 3 times; 5 dc in last ch-5 half-corner sp: half corner made; finish off.

Rnd 6: Join black in 3rd ch of beg ch-3 of prev rnd; ch 4 (counts as a trc), dc in same st: half-corner made; (dc in next dc) 18 times; in next ch-2 corner sp work (dc, trc, dc): corner made; (dc in next dc) 18 times; in next dc work (dc, trc): half-corner made; finish off and weave in all ends.

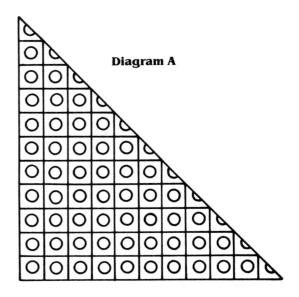

Diagram A

Assembling

Join squares as shown in Diagram A. To join squares, hold two squares with right sides tog. Carefully matching sts on both squares and with black, sew with overcast st in inner lps (see page 10) only across side, beg and ending with one corner st and being sure that all four-corner junctions are firmly joined.

Fringe

Following Fringe instructions on page 9, make single knot fringe. Cut 20″ strands of black; use 4 strands for each knot. On each shorter side of shawl, tie 3 knots evenly spaced across each square or half square and 1 knot in each joining. Trim ends evenly.

Rnds 3 and 4: Rep Rnd 2, having 2 more hdc between corners on each rnd. At end of Rnd 4: 41 hdc between corners. Finish off.

With right side of Square 2 facing you, join red in any ch-2 corner sp. Rep Rnds 1 through 4, but do not finish off. Continue with scarf center.

Scarf center

Row 1: Sl st in next hdc, ch 3 (counts as a dc), dc in next 2 hdc; (ch 1, sk next hdc, dc in next 3 hdc) 5 times; ch 4 (counts as ch-1 sp and a dc on next row), turn.

Row 2: (3 dc in next ch-1 sp, ch 1) 5 times; dc in 3rd ch of beg ch-3 of prev row; ch 3, turn.

Row 3: 2 dc in next ch-1 sp, (ch 1, 3 dc in next ch-1 sp) 5 times; ch 4 (counts as a ch-1 sp and a dc on next row), turn.

Rep Row 2 and 3 until scarf center measures 55″ (or desired length). Finish off.

Assembling

Join rem square to scarf center. To join, hold scarf center and square with right sides tog. Carefully matching sts on both pieces and with red, sew with overcast st in inner lps (see page 10) only across side, beg and ending with one corner st.

Fringe

Following Fringe instructions on page 9, make single knot fringe. Cut 18″ strands of red; use 5 strands for each knot of fringe. Tie knots every 3rd st across each short end of afghan. Trim ends evenly.

Granny Scarf

Size: About 8″ × 62″ (without fringe)

Materials: Sport weight yarn, 7 oz red; ½ oz white; ¼ oz pink; ¼ oz purple; ¼ oz lt green; ¼ oz forest green
Size D aluminum crochet hook, or size required for gauge

Gauge: 4-rnd square = 3¼″ × 3¼″
        6 dc = 1″
        3 dc rows = 1″

INSTRUCTIONS

Referring to Traditional Granny Square #1 on page 11, make two 9-rnd squares, referring to chart A for color sequence.

Border for Squares

With right side of Square 1 facing you, join red in any ch-2 corner sp.

Rnd 1: Ch 2 (counts as a hdc in this and all following rnds), 2 hdc in same sp; * hdc in each dc and ch-1 sp across square; 3 hdc in next ch-2 corner sp: corner made; rep from * 3 times more, ending last rep without working last 3 hdc: 35 hdc between 3-hdc corners; join in 2nd ch of beg ch-2. Do not turn; work in rnds.

Rnd 2: Sl st in next 2 hdc, ch 2, 2 hdc in same hdc as joining; * hdc in next 37 hdc; 3 hdc in next hdc: corner made; rep from * 3 times more, ending last rep without working last 3 hdc: 37 hdc between corners; join in 2nd of beg ch-2.

Chart A

	Square 1	Square 2
Rnd 1	Pink	Light Green
Rnd 2	White	Forest Green
Rnd 3	Purple	Pink
Rnd 4	Purple	Pink
Rnd 5	Pink	Light Green
Rnd 6	Purple	Forest Green
Rnd 7	White	Purple
Rnd 8	Pink	Purple
Rnd 9	Pink	Pink

Granny Shawl

Size: About 40″ on longest side (without fringe)

Materials: Sport weight yarn, 10 oz colors of your choice
Size E aluminum crochet hook, or size required for gauge

Gauge: 4-rnd = 3″ on shorter sides

INSTRUCTIONS

With first color choice, ch 4, join to form a ring.

Row 1 (right side): Ch 3 (counts as a dc in this and all following rows); 2 dc in ring, ch 2: corner made; 3 dc in ring; finish off.

Note: All following rows are worked with right side facing you. Do not turn at end of rows.

Row 2: Join next color in 3rd ch of beg ch-3 of prev row, ch 3, 2 dc in same st as joining: 3-dc group made; ch 1, sk next 2 dc, in ch-2 corner sp work (3 dc, ch 2, 3 dc): corner made; ch 1, sk next 2 dc, 3 dc in last dc: 3-dc group made; 1, 3-dc group on each side of corner sp; finish off.

Row 3: Join next color in 3rd ch of beg ch-3 of prev row, ch 3, 2 dc in same st as joining; ch 1, 3 dc in next ch-1 sp; ch 1, in corner sp work (3 dc, ch 2, 3 dc): corner made; ch 1, 3 dc in next ch-1 sp; ch 1, 3 dc in last dc: 2, 3-dc groups on each side of corner sp; finish off.

Row 4: Join next color in 3rd ch of beg ch-3 of prev row, ch 3, 2 dc in same st as joining; ch 1, (3 dc in next ch-1 sp, ch 1) twice; in corner sp work (3 dc, ch 2, 3 dc): corner made; ch 1, (3 dc in next ch-1 sp, ch 1) twice; 3 dc in last dc: 3, 3-dc groups on each side of corner sp; finish off.

Rep Row 4, 46 times, having one more 3-dc group on each side of corner sp on each row. Row 50: 49, 3-dc groups on each side of corner sp. Weave in all ends.

Fringe

Following Fringe instructions on page 9, make single knot fringe. Cut 20″ strands; use 4 strands for each knot. Tie knots in every sp on the two shorter sides of shawl and in the ch-2 sp at tip of shawl. Trim ends evenly.

Color Blocks Scarf, Hat, and Bag

Size: Scarf: about 6½" × 60"
Hat: about 21" around
Bag: about 13" × 13"

Materials: Sport weight yarn, 11 oz blue; 3 oz green; 3 oz yellow; 3 oz rose
Size D aluminum crochet hook, or size required for gauge (for scarf and hat)
Size E aluminum crochet hook, or size required for gauge (for bag)
Size F aluminum crochet hook, or size required for gauge (for bag)
½ yd lining fabric for bag

Gauge: With size D hook; 4-rnd square = 3¼" × 3¼"
5 hdc = 1"
5 hdc rows = 1"
With size E hook; 3 rnd square = 3¼" × 3¼"
With size F hook; 4 sc = 1"
4 sc rows = 1"

INSTRUCTIONS

SCARF
Border Squares (make 2)

Following instructions for Traditional Granny Square #2 on page 12, with smaller size hook, make eight 4-rnd squares, 2 each of green, blue, yellow and rose.

Joining

Join squares into two larger squares, each having two rows of two squares; refer to photo for placement of squares. To join squares, hold two squares with right sides tog. Carefully matching sts on both and with matching yarn, sew with overcast st in inner lps (see page 10) only across side, beg and ending with one corner st. Join in rows; then sew rows tog in same manner, being sure that all four-corner junctions are firmly joined.

Scarf center

Hold one border square with right side facing you and yellow square in upper right-hand corner. With smaller size hook, join blue in upper right-hand corner sp.

Row 1: Ch 2 (counts as a hdc), † (hdc in next 3 hdc and next ch-1 sp) 3 times, hdc in next 3 hdc, hdc in next ch-2 corner sp †; hdc in joining, hdc in next ch-2 corner sp; rep from † to † once; 35 hdc; ch 2 (counts as a hdc in following row), turn.

Row 2: Hdc between each pair of hdc; ch 2, turn.

Rep Row 2 until center measures 48".

Assembling

Join second border square to scarf in same manner as squares were joined.

Edging

Hold scarf with right side facing you and long edge at top; with smaller size hook, join blue in ch-2 corner sp in upper right-hand corner; ch 1, † (sc in next 3 dc, sc in next ch-1 sp) 3 times; sc in next 3 dc, sc in next ch-2 sp †; sc in each row of center section; sc in next ch-2 sp; rep from † to † once; finish off and weave in all ends.

Rep edging on opposite side of scarf.

Fringe

Following Fringe instructions on page 9, make single knot fringe. Cut 20" strands of blue; use 5 strands for each knot. Tie knots in every sp across each short end of scarf.

HAT
Border

Following instructions for squares in scarf instructions, with smaller size hook, make eight 4-rnd squares, 2 each of green, blue, yellow and rose.

Joining

Join squares tog in long strip, then join ends of strips tog to form a ring. Join squares in same manner as squares are joined in scarf instructions. Set aside.

Crown

With smaller size hook and blue, ch 4, join to form a ring.

Rnd 1: Ch 2 (counts as a hdc in this and all following rnds), 11 hdc in ring; join in 2nd ch of beg ch-2: 12 hdc. Do not turn; work in rnds.

Rnd 2: Sl st between next 2 hdc; ch 2, hdc in same sp; (hdc between next 2 hdc, 2 hdc between next 2 hdc) 5 times; hdc between next 2 hdc; join in 2nd ch of beg ch-2: 18 hdc.

Rnd 3: Sl st between next 2 hdc; ch 2, hdc in same sp; * (hdc between next 2 hdc) twice; 2 hdc in next hdc; rep from * 4 times more; (hdc between next 2 hdc) twice; join in 2nd ch of beg ch-2: 24 hdc.

Rnds 4 through 16: Rep Rnd 3, having one more hdc between increases on each successive rnd. At end of Rnd 16: 102 hdc.

Work even until cap measures 5½″ from center. Finish off and weave in ends.

Assembling

With blue, sew border to cap using overcast st and distributing fullness evenly.

Edging

Hold cap with right side facing you and border at top; with smaller size hook, join blue in any square joining.

Rnd 1: Ch 1, sc in same place, sc in each hdc, sp, and joining around border; join in beg sc.

Rnd 2: Ch 1, sc in same sc as joining, sc in each sc; join in beg sc.

Rnd 3: Rep Rnd 2; finish off and weave in ends.

BAG

Following instructions for Traditional Granny Square #2 on page 12, with size F hook and double strand of yarn, make thirty-two 3-rnd squares; make 8 each of green, blue, yellow, and rose.

Joining

Join squares into front and back pieces, each having 4 rows of 4 squares. Refer to Diagram A for color arrangement. Join squares in same manner as squares are joined for scarf.

Gusset

With size F hook and blue, ch 11.

Row 1: Hdc in 2nd ch from hook and in each rem ch: 10 hdc; ch 2, turn.

Row 2: Hdc in between each 2 hdc and in turning ch: 10 hdc; ch 2, turn.

Rep Row 2 until gusset measures 39″. Finish off and weave in ends.

Lining

Measure front and back pieces. Cut lining pieces to same measurements, adding a ¼″ allowance on 3 sides of each piece and a 1″ allowance on top. Cut two pieces of the lining the length of the bag plus 1¼″ by the width of the gusset plus ½″. Cut one piece of lining the width of the bag plus ½″ by the width of the gusset plus ½″. These pieces form the sides and bottom of lining.

Allow ½″ seam allowances on seams except top; top seam allowance is 1″. With right sides of lining tog, sew one long edge of side pieces to sides of front piece. With right sides tog, sew other long edge of side pieces to back piece. With wrong sides tog, sew bottom piece to bottom of front, back and side pieces. Trim seams and clip corners. With piece wrong side out, press seams to side. Turn under and baste 1″ seam allowance at top edge. Set aside.

Strap

With smaller size hook and double strand of blue, ch 6.

Row 1: Hdc in 2nd ch from hook and each rem ch: 5 hdc; ch 2, turn.

Row 2: Hdc between each 2 dc and in turning ch; ch 2, turn.

Rep Row 2 until strap measures 27″ or desired length. Finish off and weave in ends.

Assembling

Sew gusset to front and back pieces along three sides.

Top edging

Hold bag with right side facing you and opening at top. With smaller size hook, join blue in 2nd ch of upper right-hand ch-2 corner sp.

Row 1: Ch 1, sc in same st as joining; sc in each st across top; ch 1, turn.

Row 2: Sc in each sc; finish off and weave in ends.

Rep on opposite top edge.

Finishing

Sew straps securely to insides of bag, referring to photo for placement. Insert lining wrong side out. Tack to inside of bag around entire top edge. Remove basting thread.

Best Friend's Coat

Size: About 17″ × 21″

Materials: Sport weight yarn, 5 oz forest green; 1 oz lt green; ½ oz beige; ½ oz brown
Size D aluminum crochet hook, or size required for gauge

Gauge: 4-rnd square = 3½″ × 3½″
Finished square = 4″ × 4″

INSTRUCTIONS

Following instructions for Traditional Granny Square #1 on page 11, make sixteen 4-rnd squares with Color A–brown, Color B–beige, Color C–forest green, and Color D–lt green.

Square Border

Hold one square with right side facing you; join forest green in any ch-2 corner sp.

Rnd 1: Ch 2 (counts as a hdc in this and all following rnds), 2 hdc in same sp: corner made; * † (hdc between next 2 dc) twice; hdc in next ch-1 sp †; rep from † to † twice more; (hdc between next 2 hdc) twice; 3 hdc in next ch-2 corner sp: corner made; rep from * 3 times more, ending last rep without working last 3 hdc; join in 2nd ch of beg ch-2.

Rnd 2: Sl st in next hdc, ch 2, 2 hdc in same hdc: corner made; * hdc in next 13 hdc, 3 hdc in next hdc: corner made; rep from * 3 times more, ending last rep without working last 3 hdc; join in 2nd ch of beg ch-2.

Rnd 3: Sl st in next hdc, ch 2, 2 hdc in same hdc: corner made; * hdc in next 15 hdc, 3 hdc in next hdc: corner made; rep from * 3 times more, ending last rep without working last 3 hdc; join in 2nd ch of beg ch-2; finish off.

Rep with each rem square.

Following instructions for Traditional Granny Half Square on page 11, make two 4-rnd half-squares with same color sequence as 4-rnd squares.

Half Square Border

Hold half square with right side facing you and ch-2 corner sp at top; join forest green in 3rd ch of beg ch-3 of Rnd 4.

Note: Border is worked on right side.

Rnd 1: Ch 2 (counts as a hdc in this and all following rows), hdc between beg ch-3 of prev rnd and next dc, hdc between next 2 dc, hdc in ch-1 sp; † (hdc between next 2 dc) twice, hdc in ch-1 sp †; rep from † to † once more; (hdc between next 2 dc) twice; 3 hdc in ch-2 corner sp; rep from † to † 3 times; (hdc between next 2 dc) twice; hdc in last dc; finish off.

Rnd 2: Join forest green in beg ch-2 of prev row; ch 2, hdc in next 12 hdc, 3 hdc in next hdc, hdc in next 13 hdc; finish off.

Rnd 3: Join forest green in beg ch-2 of prev row; ch 2, hdc in next 13 hdc, 3 hdc in next hdc, hdc in next 14 hdc; finish off and weave in ends.

Assembling

Join squares and half squares tog as shown in Diagram A. To join squares and half squares, hold two squares or a square and a half square with right sides tog. Carefully matching sts

Diagram A

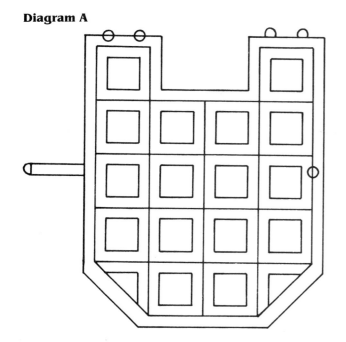

on both and with forest green, sew with overcast st in inner lps (see page 10) only across side, beg and ending with one corner st. Join in rows; then sew rows tog in same manner, being sure that all four-corner junctions are firmly joined.

Edging

Hold coat with right side facing you and front edge at top. Join forest green in center sc of upper right-hand corner.

Rnd 1: Ch 2 (counts as a hdc in this and all following rnds), 2 hdc in same hdc; hdc in each hdc around coat, working 3 hdc in each center hdc of each rem outer corner and skipping one hdc in each corner of inside neck edge; join in 2nd ch of beg ch-2.

Rnd 2: Ch 2, 3 hdc in next hdc; hdc in each hdc, working 3 hdc in each center hdc of each rem outer corner and skipping one hdc in each corner of inside neck edge; join in 2nd of beg ch-2.

Rnd 3: Rep Rnd 2. Finish off and weave in ends.

Finishing

Sew 2 buttons to left front edge and 1 button to right side, referring to Diagram A for placement. Crochet buttonholes on right front edge as follows.

Hold coat with right side facing you and front edge at top. Join forest green in center hdc of upper right-hand corner of right front edge.

Row 1: Ch 1, sc in next 4 hdc, ch 6, sk next 4 hdc, sc in next 5 hdc; ch 6, sk next 4 hdc, sc in next 5 hdc, ch 1, turn.

Row 2: Sc in next 5 sc, 4 sc in next ch-6 lp; sc in next 5 sc, 4 sc in next ch-6 lp, sc in rem sc; finish off and weave in ends.

Side Strap

Ch 12.

Row 1: Hdc in 3rd ch from hook and each rem ch: 10 hdc; ch 2, turn.

Row 2: Hdc in each hdc; ch 2, turn.

Rep Row 2 until strap measures 5″.

Next Row: Hdc in next hdc, ch 10, hdc in last hdc; ch 1, turn.

Last Row: Sc in next hdc, 8 sc in ch-10 lp, sc in last hdc; finish off and weave in ends.

Sew strap to left side matching placement with button on right side.

Log Cabin Slippers

Sizes:	Medium	Large
Finished Slipper Length	9″	10″

Materials: Worsted weight yarn, 3 oz (183 yds) in various colors; for Medium size

Size E aluminum crochet hook (for Size Large, Size F aluminum crochet hook), or size required for gauge

Gauge: For Medium Size, Log Cabin Square = 4½″ (point to point)

For Large Size, Log Cabin Square = 5″ (point to point)

Log Cabin Square

Ch 4, join to form a ring.

Rnd 1: Work 8 sc in ring: 8 sc. Note: In this and all following rnds, do not join. Mark beg st of each rnd.

Rnd 2: * 3 sc in next sc: corner made, sc in next sc; rep from * 3 times more: 16 sc.

Rnd 3: Sc in next sc; * in next sc, work corner; sc in next 3 sc; rep from * 2 times more; in next sc, work corner; sc in next sc; drawing through new color, sc in next sc: 24 sc.

Rnd 4: Sc in next 2 sc; * in next sc, work corner; sc in next 5 sc; rep from * 2 times more; in next sc, work corner; sc in next 3 sc: 32 sc.

Rnd 5: Sc in next 3 sc; * in next sc, work corner; sc in next 7 sc; rep from * 2 times more; in next sc, work corner; sc in next 3 sc; drawing through new color, sc in next sc: 40 sc.

Rnd 6: Sc in next 4 sc; * in next sc, work corner; sc in next 9 sc; rep from * 2 times more; in next sc, work corner; sc in next 5 sc: 48 sc.

Rnd 7: Sc in next 5 sc; * in next sc, work corner; sc in next 11 sc; rep from * 2 times more; in next sc, work corner; sc in next 5 sc; drawing through new color, sc in next sc: 56 sc.

Rnd 8: Sc in next 6 sc; * in next sc, work corner; sc in next 13 sc; rep from * 2 times more; in next sc, work corner; sc in next 7 sc: 64 sc.

Rnd 9: Sc in next 7 sc; * in next sc, work corner; sc in next 15 sc; rep from * 2 times more; in next sc, work corner; sc in next 8 sc: 72 sc; join in first sc; finish off and weave in ends.

INSTRUCTIONS

Using hook giving correct gauge for size desired, make 6 Log Cabin squares.

Finishing

Hold 2 squares with wrong sides tog. Carefully matching sts, sew with overcast st in inner lps only (page 10) in each st across ending in opposite corner and referring to Diagram A for arrangement of squares to form Slipper Base. Sew rem squares of Slipper Base tog in same manner as above. With wrong sides tog, place one square (Square #5, Diagram B) on Slipper Base and match edges A and B as per Diagrams A and

Diagram A　　　　　**Slipper Base**

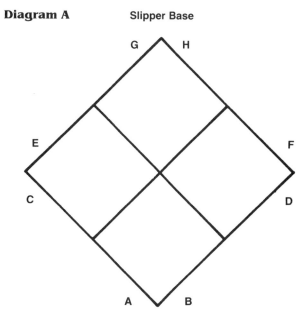

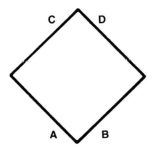

Diagram B
Square 5

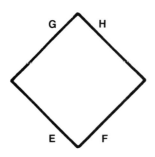

Diagram C
Square 6

B. Sew edges A and B tog in same manner. Match edges C and D of Square #5 and Slipper Base and sew tog in same manner. With wrong sides tog, place one square (Square #6, Diagram C) on Slipper Base and match edges G and H as per Diagrams A and C. Sew edges G and H of Square #6 and Slipper Base tog in same manner. Do not sew edges E and F of Square #6 and Slipper Base, as this is the slipper foot opening. Finish off and weave in ends.

Granny's Ring Slippers

Sizes:	Small	Medium	Large
Finished Slipper Length	8″	9″	10″

Materials: Worsted weight yarn, 2 oz (122 yds) in various colors; for Size Small, Size G aluminum crochet hook (for Size Medium, Size I aluminum crochet hook; for Size Large, Size K aluminum crochet hook), or size required for gauge.

Gauge: For Size Small, Granny's Ring = 4″ (point to point)
For Size Medium, Granny's Ring = 4½″ (point to point)
For Size Large, Granny's Ring = 5″ (point to point)

Granny Ring Square

Ch 4, join to form a ring.

Rnd 1: Ch 3 (counts as first dc), work 15 dc in ring: 16 dc; join in 3rd ch of beg ch-3; finish off.

Rnd 2: Join new color in any dc; ch 3 (counts as first dc), dc in same joining st; 2 dc in each dc; join in 3rd ch of beg ch-3: 32 dc; finish off.

Rnd 3: Join new color in any dc, ch 1, sc in same joining st; sc in each dc; join in first sc: 32 sc.

Rnd 4: Ch 3 (counts as first dc), in same joining st, work dc, ch 1, 2 dc: beg corner made; * † hdc in next 2 sc, sc in next 3 sc, hdc in next 2 sc †; in next sc, work 2 dc, ch 1, 2 dc: corner made; rep from * twice; rep from † to † once; join in 3rd ch of beg ch-3: 44 sts and 4 ch-1 sps.

INSTRUCTIONS

Using hook giving correct gauge for size desired, make 6 Granny Ring squares.

Finishing

Work same as Finishing for Log Cabin Slippers on page 139.

Sunflower Tote

Size: About 12″ × 15″

Materials: Worsted weight yarn, 5 oz navy; 7 oz colors of your choice
Size F aluminum crochet hook, or size required for gauge

Gauge: One square = 3″ × 3″

INSTRUCTIONS

Sunflower Square (make 40)

(**NOTE:** Use navy only where noted.)

With color A, ch 4; join to form a ring.

Rnd 1: Ch 3 (counts as dc), 15 dc in ring: 16 dc; join in 3rd ch of beg ch-3; finish off.

Rnd 2: Join color B with sl st in any dc, ch 4 (counts as dc, ch 1); (dc in next dc, ch 1) 15 times; join in 3rd ch of beg ch-4: 16 ch-1 sps; finish off.

Rnd 3: Join color C in any ch-1 sp, ch 3 (counts as dc), in same sp work (dc, ch 2, 2 dc): corner made, * † (sk next dc, sc in next ch-1 sp, ch 1) 3 times †; sk next dc, in next ch-1 sp work (2 dc, ch 2, 2 dc): corner made; rep from * twice more, then rep from † to † once; sk next dc; join in 3rd ch of beg ch-3: 4 corners; finish off.

Rnd 4: Join navy in any ch-2 corner sp, ch 1, 2 sc in same sp; * † sc between next 2 dc, (sc in next ch-1 sp, sk next dc) 3 times; sc in next ch-1 sp, sc between next 2 dc †, 3 sc in next ch-2 corner sp; rep from * twice more, then rep from † to † once; join in beg ch-1; finish off.

Joining

For front piece, join 20 squares in 5 rows of 4 squares. To join squares, hold two squares with right sides tog. Carefully matching sts on both squares and with navy, sew with overcast st in inner lps (see page 10) only across side, beg and ending with one corner st. Join squares in rows; then sew rows tog in same manner, being sure that all four-corner junctions are firmly joined.

Rep for back section.

Gusset

With navy, ch 8.

Row 1: Sc in 2nd ch from hook and each rem ch: 7 sc; ch 1, turn.

Row 2: Sc in each sc, ch 1, turn.

Rep Row 2 until gusset measures 42″ or the length of sides A, B, and C (Diagram A). Finish off and weave in ends.

Handles (make 2)

With navy, ch 5.

Row 1: Sc in 2nd ch from hook and each rem ch: 4 sc; ch 1, turn.

Row 2: Sc in each sc; ch 1, turn.

Rep Row 2 until handle measures 20″. Finish off and weave in ends.

Assembling

Referring to Diagram A for placement, sew front and back pieces to gusset with overcast st. Sew straps firmly to inside of bag, referring to Diagram A for placement.

Edging

Hold bag with right side of front facing you; join navy in center sc of upper right-hand corner; * sk next 2 sc, 5 dc in next sc, sk next 2 sc, sl st in next sc; rep from * around top edge, adjusting sts so that last rep ends with sl st in beg sl st. Finish off and weave in ends.

Diagram A

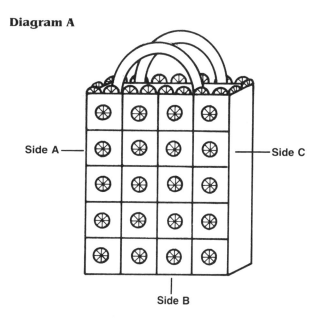

141

INDEX

Bold numbers indicate location of color photo